Tea on the TITANIC

100 Years Later

Penelope Carlevato

outskirtspress
DENVER, COLORADO

Tea on The Titanic
100 Years Later

v2.0 r1.2

Outskirts Press, Inc.
http://www.outskirtspress.com

ISBN: 978-1-4327-9199-5

PRINTED IN THE UNITED STATES OF AMERICA

Table of Contents

Chapter I
A Nautical Beginning

As a young girl, I had a wonderful opportunity to travel on the world's fastest ocean liner, the S.S. United States, from New York to Southampton, England. It was a floating luxury hotel with swimming pools, bowling alleys, shops, restaurants, playgrounds and theaters, much like the fabled *Titanic*. The most impressive memory I have of that trip is an afternoon tea with my mother. The tea service on the ship was impeccable; tables covered in starched white linens, tea poured from gleaming silver teapots, and delightful tarts, cakes and scones. My English mother was extremely pleased that an American ship could provide such an accurate presentation of afternoon tea. Until that time, our little tea parties together were at home, so this was a memorable event - "tea at sea!"

The ritual of afternoon tea has been popular with cultured society for many years. The properly set tea table, resplendent with linen tablecloths, fine English bone china teacups and teapots, silver sugar tongs, sugar cubes, dainty cucumber sandwiches and buttery shortbread, offers a much needed opportunity to come away from the busyness of life and connect with friends and family. Afternoon tea is a restful interlude that can comfort the harried soul in any era, those in 1912 and in 2012.

When our family arrived in Southampton, we traveled to Waterloo Station by train just as those passengers on the *Titanic* did more than half a century before us. I think our voyage on the new ocean liner, the S. S. United States and the trip on the train were the beginning of my interest in the history of the *Titanic*.

The demise of the *Titanic* is a story that has been told many times… in movies, books, and newspapers. The recent accident of the cruise ship *Costa Concordia* off the coast of Italy has attracted much media coverage. Many people have said it reminded them of the *Titanic*. Even though ship travel has advanced in many ways over the past 100 years, panic and chaos were evident as evacuation began from the *Costa Concordia*. The 114,500-ton ship is the largest passenger liner ever to sink (two and a half times the *Titanic*'s tonnage of 46,000 tons). It hit a rock; the underside of the ship was flooded with water; and it began to sink. The chief executive of the cruise line, Pier Luigi Foschi, stated, "these ships are ultra-safe. It is an exceptional event, which was unforeseeable." Was he saying the *Costa Concordia* was also "unsinkable"? Will this sinking be as talked about in 100 years as is *The Titanic*? Time will tell.

The popular PBS series, "Downton Abbey," on Masterpiece Theater, is a fictional drama that follows the lives of an aristocratic family and their servants in the Edwardian era. The first episode opens with the news of the sinking of the *Titanic* and the loss of future heirs. The household, family and servants alike, is devastated by the news. They, too, thought the *Titanic* unsinkable. While no scenes actually were filmed on a set depicting the *Titanic*, the attention to detail in clothing, etiquette, formality, and class distinction is extremely authentic. Proper serving of afternoon tea and dinner are matters of utmost importance to any hostess, and the butler does his job with perfection.

The RMS (Royal Mail Steamship) *Titanic* is probably the most famous ship ever built. It certainly was the most famous ship ever to sink. The *Titanic* and her sister ship, the *Olympic*, were the "air buses" of the day. The captain and the crew were the most experienced and competent sailors in all of Great Britain. Constructed to impress and attract the world's most elite travelers, the *Titanic*'s maiden and only voyage had some of the world's richest and most famous people aboard:

John Jacob Astor and his pregnant 19-year-old wife Madeleine, who had left America for a few months to escape public controversy certain to surround his choice of a child bride; Margaret "Molly" Brown, the Colorado millionairess, who needed to rush home to be with her sick grandson; Sir Cosmos Duff-Gordon and his wife, the famous British fashion designer Lady Lucile Duff-Gordon, creator of the "Lucile Dress Salons" in London, Paris and New York; George and Eleanor Widener of the Philadelphia Railway System and their twenty-seven-year-old son, Harry; popular writer Jacques Futrelle and his wife, Lily May; Walter Douglas, director of The Quaker Oats Company, and his wife Mary Helen; and Major Archie Butt, the ship's most famous bachelor, and Military Aide to President William Howard Taft and, formerly, to President Theodore Roosevelt, and beloved friend of both.

A British ship, such as the *Titanic*, served afternoon tea around 4:00 p.m. Those passengers in first- and second-class would experience tea similar to my experience on the S. S. United States. The third-class passengers had "high tea," or their evening meal. Because the third-class were working people, such as shopkeepers, miners and laborers, who did not have the luxury of stopping for a tea party in mid-afternoon. Their meal, or tea, would be taken at a kitchen, or high table, thus the term "high tea." Not to be confused with afternoon tea, high tea would have been a substantial meal, consisting of a meat dish, potatoes and the proverbial pot of tea. Afternoon tea consists of dainty tea sandwiches (with the crusts removed), scones with jam and clotted cream, pastries or sweets and a pot of tea, a very social affair.

Those who enjoyed lavish lifestyles, without concern for the cost, comprised the first-class passengers of this opulent floating hotel. The *Titanic*, as grand as any five-star hotel, certainly satisfied their obsession with all things opulent, especially the fine dining. Afternoon tea would have been one of the prized social events of the day, with many of Lady Duff-Gordon's fabulous "tea-dresses" worn by the socialites. The ladies on board would have dressed in the latest Paris and London gowns, and hats adorned with lace, pearls, feathers, ribbons and satin. As they gathered for afternoon tea in the sitting rooms of their suites, or the Verandah, Palm Court or Café Parisie, they sipped tea and enjoyed dainty tea foods. Their conversation most likely centered on fashion, the theater or the next social event they would attend when back in New York.

The passengers on this ship all had high expectations of their journey across the Atlantic. The first- and second-class were expecting a carefree and enjoyable vacation; the third-class the promise of a new way of life in America. Following the protocol of the day, the three classes of passengers would have been kept entirely separate, and signs were posted at every entrance to the three classes of accommodation. This would require the ship to have three separate dining rooms, lounges, and promenade decks. The first-class suites and accommodations were the very pinnacle of luxury and attracted the nobility and aristocracy of the day. The majority (more than 700) of the passengers on the *Titanic* were Irish immigrants traveling in third-class and going to America for a better life. Many had said good-bye to their families for the last time, with all their possessions in a large bag or steamer trunk. Many were leaving Ireland because of unemployment and the dismal economy in Ireland. White Star shipping lines saw the steerage passenger as a quick way of making money. The cost of a ticket on the *Titanic* for first-class was about $4400.00 or $88,000 in today's economy, and third-class was about $40.00, or $800.00 today. The White Star Line made the steerage accommodations much nicer than other ships traveling the same route, so they were able to set sail with no vacancies on the lower decks.

Our family traveled on the second crossing of the S. S. United States, from New York to Southampton. On its maiden voyage, just a week earlier, the ship broke the speed record formerly held by the Queen Mary, a Cunard vessel. Speed was the driving force for most ships in the 1950s as it was in 1912. Our trip took about 3 1/2 days, compared to 10 days if the *Titanic* had completed her voyage. The White Star Line was establishing its reputation, first by building the *Olympic*, then the *Titanic*. Built by Harland and Wolff of Belfast, Ireland, the *Titanic* was the largest passenger steamship of its day; four thousand laborers worked on its construction over more than three years, many of them laboring 50 to 60 hours a week. White Star's dedication was due to its desire for greater market share in the shipping and passenger industry. Consequently, they named their ships to suggest the biggest, best, and fastest – affixing the suffix "ic" to each ship's name...*Titanic*, *Olympic*, *Britannic*. Their competitors, the Cunard line, boasted two prestigious ships: the *Lusitania* and *The Maretania*, which were luring potential passengers. J. Bruce Ismay, the chairman and general manager of the White Star Line, saw his company losing market dominance, so he arranged with Harland and Wolff not to build ships for any other company than White Star.

The conception of the *Titanic* was Mr. Ismay's; Thomas Andrews, managing director and head of the drafting department at Harland and Wolff, was its chief designer. He was a perfectionist and knew every inch of every ship he designed. His custom was to go on each maiden voyage and make sure that everything was in optimal working order. Before the completion of the *Titanic*, Mr. Andrews urged the owners to install 36 lifeboats and a double hull with watertight compartments all the way up to B deck, but he was overruled. After the Belfast-Southampton leg with his engineering team, Andrews remarked to a friend that the ship was "nearly as perfect as human brains can make her." He arranged to continue with the ship to New York.

The *Titanic* was widely considered unsinkable. It was fitted with 20 lifeboats, enough to carry 52 percent of the passengers. The capacity (crew and passengers) was 2207. This anomaly –why an insufficient number of lifeboats? – is explained by that fact that the *Titanic* was within the legal requirements of Board of Trade regulations, which required any ship over 10,000 tons to carry 16 lifeboats. The regulation was overdue for correction, as most of the large ships, including the *Titanic,* were more than 45,000 tons. The ship set sail, however, from Southampton on April 10th at noon with its first passengers on board. Most of these had traveled by train on the "*Titanic Specia*l" boat train from Waterloo Station in London. She made port calls at Cherbourg, France, at about 6:30 p.m.; and then traveled on to Queenstown (now the port of Cobh, County Cork), Ireland, arriving midday. From there the cruise to America would begin.

The world of 1912 was a time of great optimism, success, luxury, and amazing technological advances: the focus was on life becoming bigger and better. The Industrial Revolution and many scientific discoveries and inventions were changing the world. The *Titanic* was a symbol of all these changes. English and American societies were free of the stuffy and somewhat Puritanical manners of the Victorian Era (the Queen herself had died after more than six decades on the throne, in 1901). The following "Edwardian Era" was marked by freer attitudes and more enjoyment of social life. But never did the nobility or upper classes surrender their prerogatives of opulent "lifestyles of the rich and famous." The distinctions between the classes remained strong: rich *vs.* poor; women *vs.* men; crew *vs.* passengers. First class, Second Class, and Third Class (steerage) all had their own defining aspects and boundaries. An ocean liner in the Edwardian years was a microcosm of society.

The night skies of April 14th were clear. The Titanic was four days at sea and proceeding at 22-1/2 knots (approximately 23–25 mph) toward what was to be the completion of its maiden voyage. The sea was extremely calm. Captain Edward Smith had received several wire messages from ships in the area that icebergs had been sighted. With his long experience of 32 years as an employee of the White Star Lines, he acknowledged the warnings and even sent a lookout to watch for the icebergs. But he took no further action. At 11:40 p.m. the lookout rang the crow's nest bell three times, the danger signal and called the bridge. "Iceberg ahead!" he cried.

But by then, the iceberg could not be avoided. The *Titanic*'s starboard side scraped the iceberg, and the ship began to take on water immediately. The passengers did not know the extent of the damage, and many were lulled into believing all was well. Thomas Andrews, of Harland and Wolfe, was on the ship and knew instantly, when he surveyed the damage, that the *Titanic* had, at the most, two hours to stay afloat.

As the passengers began to gather topside, a sense of urgency overcame them. Lifeboats were being lowered and the call for "women and children to the lifeboats, men stand back from the boats" was ordered. Many men would give their lives so women and children could find places on the lifeboats, but there were other men who dressed as women, or shoved and pushed their way into lifeboats, desperate to survive. J. Bruce Ismay, Chairman of the White Star Line was one of these. Suddenly thrown together, members of different classes, rich and poor, masters and servants, many different nationalities, some not speaking or understanding English, insured that chaos was inevitable during the last few hours of the voyage.

Ship's musicians played throughout those hours. They began with rousing songs, such as *Alexander's Rag Time Band*, and continued with the last song, reportedly, the hymn *Nearer My God to Thee.* They actually were two different groups that performed in different places and at different times during the voyage. The Director, Wallace Hartley, had a group of four, which usually entertained the guests at teatime and after-dinner concerts. Three other musicians usually were stationed outside the restaurant. That fateful night was probably the first time they all played together. They will always be remembered as a very striking example of those who bravely stay the course, who nobly "go down with the ship."

The Third-Class passengers were not under any illusion that the ship was all right. At least, they were able to know the horrible truth sooner than above decks. Being lower in the ship, they early saw water swirling on their deck, in their hallways, and in the cabins. Many of these steerage passengers were not allowed to go up on deck and waited below for instructions to proceed up. With only 16 lifeboats and several rafts on board, more than half the passengers had no place to go. At 2:20 a.m., little more than two hours after the iceberg had been hit, only 705 passengers and crew were in lifeboats whose capacities were 1,200 people. More than 1,500 men, women and children were left on the ship.

The *Titanic* suddenly lurched upward with the bow pointing toward heaven. She remained that way for several minutes. Then her lights went out, came on again for just a second, and then went out for the last time. A horrible noise ripped through the cold air as engines and boilers ripped from their mounts. Then the *Titanic* slowly began to sink.

Passengers in the lifeboats prepared for a huge vortex of suction, rowing as fast as they could, as the boat began its plunge to the bottom of the ocean, but it never happened. Cries of people in the water who had been thrown from the deck lasted only a few minutes. The water temperature was only 28°F. Some people who clung to floating debris lasted longer than others, but within about 40 minutes, there was only silence under the stars.

About 4:30 a.m., survivors saw the lights of the Cunard ship, Carpathia. The vessel arrived at the scene and picked up 705 survivors over a four-hour period. Lifeboats, debris, and floating bodies covered a four square-mile area. Captain Arthur Rostron of the Carpathia had responded quickly when informed of the *Titanic*'s emergency. When Captain Smith inquired about the time estimate for the Carpathia to reach the *Titanic*'s location, Captain Rostron calculated that four hours would be required to sail the 58 miles. Captain Smith knew by then the *Titanic* would be gone. Captain Rostron turned his ship around from its intended route and had the crew prepare to receive the survivors. The captain ran the Carpathia at nearly full speed in order to reach the *Titanic* as soon as possible. When asked later by a reporter about the safety of going that fast through a field of icebergs, Captain Rostron told him "someone else's hand other than mine was on the wheel that night."

The *Titanic* was equipped with a state-of-the-art Marconi Radio transmitter, but most ships, including the *Titanic,* weren't convinced having a transmitter was really a necessity, especially keeping it manned 24 hours a day. It was used as a novelty for passengers to send messages to family and friends. At 12:15 a.m., 35 minutes after the ship had hit the iceberg, Captain Smith told the radio operators to send out a call for assistance. One of the men asked Captain Smith if they should send out the international call for distress. "Yes, at once," and handed him the ship's current position on a piece of paper. Several ships responded but were too far away to help. The radio operators aboard the *Titanic* used the new code for distress for the first time: SOS. Meanwhile, a ship much closer than the Carpathia, the Californian, was only about 20 miles away, but was not responding to the call for help. Even with flares and rockets being shot off the ship's deck, the Californian did not respond. If this ship had come to the *Titanic's* aid, many of the passengers would have survived. Later it was reported that the crew aboard the Californian thought the rockets being fired from the *Titanic* were some sort of company signal; in any event the ship, quite aware of the ice fields, decided to stop and spend the night and proceed in daylight. The Federal Radio Act of 1912, which provides for a separate frequency of distress calls and 24-hour transmission service for all ships at sea, is part of the legacy of the tragic mistakes of that fateful April night.

When visiting the "*Titanic* Experience," an exhibition in Tennessee, one can see a mock- up of the deck, complete with a "growing iceberg," a trough filled with water at 28°F, and an ambient temperature of 32°F, the conditions that existed on April 14th. I put my hand into the water and could only keep it there for a few seconds. The experience of being in a situation very like the *Titanic*'s passengers of that fateful night was dreadful. I cannot imagine the terror of those who clung to deck chairs, life preservers, pieces of wood, or even those in the lifeboats as they drifted in the frigid and dark night. The experience made it seem all the more real and heartbreaking.

The trip to this exhibition was a reminder that nothing, or no one, is unsinkable. Could the *Titanic*'s collision with the iceberg have been avoided? Several things seem apparent after this horrible tragedy. Although Captain Smith remained with his ship and did not desert his duty as commander, he had been overconfident. He had received warnings, in fact several warnings, from other ships about icebergs in the area. The *Titanic*'s speed was too fast in an area of ice fields, and since the ship had never gone through emergency drills, he was unprepared for the contingency of the ship needing to stop or turn.

We all can look back and wonder why such a great ship sank when it was built as "unsinkable," and we all could benefit by remembering that "man may plan his ways, but it is God who directs our steps."

"There are many types of ships. There are wooden ships, and metal ships, and ships that sail the sea. But the best are friendships, and may they always be."
Old Irish Quote

Chapter 2
History and Tradition of Tea

"Wouldn't it be dreadful to live in a country where they didn't have tea?"
Noel Coward

The pleasure of drinking tea dates back about 5,000 years. There are two interesting legends regarding the discovery of tea. One tells the story of a Chinese Emperor named Shen Nung, who was sitting under a tree boiling water for purification. A gust of wind blew leaves into his kettle and greatly improved the taste of the water. The Emperor enjoyed his first cup of tea. The second legend gives the discovery to a Buddhist monk from India. He was traveling in China to begin nine years of meditation. During his fifth year, he suffered a time of great fatigue and was finding it impossible to continue. He chewed some twigs and leaves from a nearby tree and at once he was restored. Whatever the truth behind either of these legends, tea has become a favored part of peoples' lives, and every aspect of the flavorful leaves is interesting.

The leaves that revitalize and restore health are from the *Camellia Senesis* bush, a member of the evergreen family that thrives best in fertile hilly regions. Tea bushes are grown on plantations or estates in approximately forty countries. India is by far the world's largest producer and exporter of tea. The plant, with its shiny green leaves, takes about five years to develop, but then can be harvested several times a month. Only the tip and the top two leaves of the youngest shoots are picked. These freshly picked leaves are spread out on trays in shaded sheds, allowing moisture to evaporate from the leaves. The leaves are then exposed to heat and go through a process of fermentation or oxidation, producing changes in color and fragrance. The leaves are sorted through a series of screens, beginning with large openings and continuing to a very fine mesh. The larger tea leaves usually produce the better grade of tea. The smallest leaves are called "dust" or "fannings" and are used in tea bags.

There are four main types of tea, all coming from the same plant, the Camellia Sinesis:

- White Tea - very little processing, picked once a year, light sweet taste.
- Green Tea - unfermented (not exposed to heat), delicate taste and light green color.
- Oolong Tea - semi-fermented, cross between black and green tea in color and taste.
- Black Tea - fully fermented, yields a hearty flavor and darker brew; the most popular tea.

Tea is very economical, yielding 300 cups of tea per pound, and is second to water as the most consumed beverage in the world. It is one of the few drinks that has no sodium, no fat, no carbohydrates, no sugar, and no calories. Tea must contain leaves from the Camellia Senesis plant in order to be called "tea." Herbal "teas" are products of fruits, flowers, leaves, bark, seeds, or roots from plants other than the tea plant. These drinks are tisanes or infusions, and are usually caffeine free. All tea from the Camellia Senesis bush, including green tea, has caffeine.

While tea had great popularity in the East, it did not arrive in Europe until the mid-1600s and was first served at a coffee house in

London. In England, it quickly replaced the national drink of ale. Tea mania had arrived! A traditional afternoon tea ceremony dates back 150 years to Victorian England, then continued into the Edwardian era and is still popular today. We can thank Anna, the 7th Duchess of Bedford, and Queen Victoria's lady in waiting, who popularized the delightful art of afternoon tea in the mid-1800s. Since dinner was served late, Anna began to have "a sinking feeling" (hypoglycemia?) mid-afternoon. She asked her servants to bring a tray with tea and cakes to her sitting room. The nourishment gave her a much needed energy boost and kept her energized until the dinner hour. This little snack quickly became a popular pastime within her circle of friends, and the tradition of afternoon tea spread throughout the British aristocracy.

Queen Victoria carried on this ritual and began to give lavish afternoon tea parties in the garden at Buckingham Palace. The reason many afternoon teas today are called "Victorian Teas" is from this association with Queen Victoria. Every summer, Queen Elizabeth II keeps this tradition alive by holding three afternoon teas in the Rose Garden at Buckingham Palace, and one at Holyrood House in Edinburgh. The invited guests, over 8,000 per event, are those Brits who have served England well in numerous capacities. They start arriving at the palace around 3:00 p.m. and mingle in the garden drinking more than 27,000 cups of tea. Every year about 32,000 British citizens receive a hand-written invitation to attend the garden tea from the Lord Chamberlain's office at Buckingham Palace. It is impossible to request admission to one of the parties, as one must be appointed by a royal approved sponsor. The Queen and the Duke of Edinburgh, with other members of the Royal Family, arrive at 4:00 p.m. and circulate among the guests for several hours. The Lyons Tea Company originally created a special tea blend just for the palace parties, called Maison Lyons Tea. A blend of Darjeeling and Assam and said to have a flavor resembling peaches or very sweet Muscat grapes. It is still served at each tea. Twinings Tea Company took over the Lyons Tea Company in the

1920s and continues to blend this special tea for the royal event.

Garden Party Tips for Attendees:

1. Clothing: Morning Dress or Lounge Suits for men; Afternoon dress, comfortable shoes, umbrella and hat for women – no pants, please!
2. Go to the Loo before entering the garden. Portable loos are available, but there will be 8,000 others in attendance!
3. Ladies, curtsey (bending the knees with one foot in front of the other) if you meet the Queen; Gentlemen, bow from the neck, down. Do not shake hands with the Queen unless she offers her hand first.
4. Do not engage in conversation with the Queen unless she speaks to you first.
5. Be prepared to leave when the Queen and her family enter the palace. The Garden Party is over.

Together with the *Titanic's* 100-year anniversary, Queen Elizabeth celebrates her Diamond Jubilee, 60 years on the throne, in 2012. She is the second-longest reigning monarch in the British Empire (Queen Victoria ruled the country for 64 years). Many celebrations are planned; the annual Palace garden teas should be spectacular.

In Victorian times tea was very expensive and usually kept in a tea caddy, a locked wooden or tin box that held two or three types of tea. A tea caddy was of great importance in the household, as tea blending was usually done in each home, instead of commercially prepared as is done today. Most of the tea caddies had three containers inside: one for black tea, one for green tea, and the third for blending the two teas. The lady of the house kept a key to the caddy on a chain or ribbon around her neck to keep the servants from using the "good" tea. As tea became more popular and affordable, the use of a tea caddy diminished, and today is more of a collectible item than a necessity.

It is hard to believe that barely a hundred years ago, tea was only for the wealthy or royalty in Western societies. Today, it is a daily beverage of millions. Instead of keeping the classes separated by having tea in private dining quarters, teatime is a great way to bring friends together and to grow relationships. As wonderful as it is to have tea in lovely hotels, on cruise ships, tearooms, and up-scale restaurants, nothing is more pleasant than having friends for tea in your home. Afternoon tea settings with many different themes and recipes are provided in other chapters of this book.

My great-grandparents lived in the northeast of England, and had a business providing household help to wealthy families near Sandringham, the country retreat of the royal family. Queen Mary, the grandmother of Queen Elizabeth II, called at their home to discuss the employment of several housemaids. My great grandmother, never to be taken by surprise by anyone, including the Queen, quickly brought the tea trolley into the parlor and made the Queen a cup of tea. A wooden tea caddy on the trolley contained her special blend of tea. Several years ago, I received that tea caddy from a family member, who knew I would be thrilled to own such a royal treasure. I actually met Queen Mary at a carpentry shop on the grounds of Sandringham when our family visited in the 1950s. We talked with her for about 15 minutes. Among the things she discussed was her son, the former King Edward VIII, who had married an American, Wallis Simpson. She wanted to know where Mother was from in England, where we lived in America, how far was that from New York, did we like New York (where her son lived). My mother, a staunch royalist, was overjoyed to have this story to tell at home. Whenever one goes to England, one is asked, "Are you going to visit the Queen?" Had I known the story of the tea caddy at that time, I would have asked for details and discussed it with Queen Mary. From that moment on, whenever I had "show and tell" at school, I always shared my visit with the Queen.

Queen Mary
A picture taken by my mother at Sandringham

Tea on the *Titanic* would have been very similar to the teas given by Queen Victoria. The table would have been an impressive sight with the White Star China, linen napkins, silver teaspoons, and the food most likely served on silver tiers. Flavored teas were not popular at that time, so a black tea, Darjeeling, or Earl Grey would have been the choices. Because the *Titanic* made dining and service high priorities, nothing would have been left to chance. The afternoon tea would have been planned before the ship ever set sail. Fresh-baked scones, served with the traditional clotted cream and jam; fresh fruit tartlets; and crisp buttery shortbread would have been carefully arranged.

Every tea company employs a tea-blender, each with his own recipes for a variety of teas. The skill of the tea blender ensures that the taste of the tea will be the same with each batch. Some of the blends may contain as many as 30 different teas. An English breakfast tea from one company may taste very different from another of the same name, because of the recipe used by the tea-blender. The following is a list of tea-tasting terms that distinguish one tea from another and how the tea-blender would classify a tea:

Appearance: Tippy; Wiry; Stalky; Dull; Bright
Taste: Bright; Plain; Malty; Liquor; Body; Soft

Earl Grey is probably the most popular tea blend. Its name conjures an image of something quite royal. It is named after the 2nd Earl Grey, who was Prime Minister of England from 1830 to 1834. The legend credits a Mandarin Chinese man who gave the tea or a recipe for the tea to the Earl as a gift for saving his son's life. Twinings Tea and Jackson's of Piccadilly claim that they have the original Earl Grey tea recipe. A traditional Earl Grey blend will have a medium strength of black tea flavored with the oil of Bergamont (a small pear-shaped fruit grown in Italy, similar to an orange, but with a very distinctive taste). The flavor of tea varies according to producer and recipe, as well as the area of the leaves' growth, much like wine.

"I love to mix teas. My favorite blend of tea is half Earl Grey and half Lapsong Suchoung,"
Sarah, The Duchess of York

Flavored teas were not sold commercially until about 1945. Now every tea company has hundreds of varieties. Many are flavored with oils, real fruits, leaves, or flowers all providing an abundance of choices. There are teas for every kind of social occasion, from a child's tea to the tea served at the boardroom to a group of businessmen. But it all goes back to taking time to sit down with others and have a cup of tea.

During the Edwardian era, tea was only available as loose tea. In 1908, Thomas Sullivan, a tea importer in New York, began to send out his tea samples in little silk pouches instead of tins to reduce his cost. He soon began to get increased orders, but he was rather confused when the customers complained that the tea was not arriving in the little bags, but still in the loose-leaf form. Slowly the tea industry began the business of selling tea in tea bags. Today the majority of tea sold worldwide is tea bags. As popular as tea bags are, tea made with loose-leaf tea is superior in taste. I know I will be challenged on this point, but the proof is in the "pudding!" If you are a coffee drinker, may I use the analogy of drinking instant coffee or fresh brewed coffee. Or fresh peas and canned peas? There is a big difference.

Iced tea is very common in our culture and accounts for 80 to 85% of tea consumed in America. It usually is a summer-time drink and is even served at afternoon teas in America. It became popular during the World's Fair in St. Louis in 1904. The weather was very warm and humid, and hot tea wasn't selling well. A tea merchant borrowed some ice from the neighboring ice cream vendor and soon had a long line of customers for his cool drink. I will never forget the first time my English cousins ordered tea while visiting us in California. A look of confusion came over them as the waitress placed a tall glass of iced tea on the table. We all had a good laugh as we explained the need to mention "hot" when placing your order. When purchasing a cup of tea in England, it will be served hot and the waitress will ask if you want it black or white; black has no milk; white is served with milk. One more word about iced tea...Southern sweet iced tea. This is served all year round in all the southern states and is very, very, sweet. Since iced tea frequently is a summer-time drink north of the Mason Dixon line, it seems strange that in the south, sweet tea is popular all year round. When our family lived in Tennessee, I began to have friends over for afternoon tea. Very few had ever had hot tea. It was such an enjoyable treat to introduce them to a cup of hot tea, and of course I had them try it *white.*

Tea is not just a tradition in England; it is a way of life. I hope you will be able to envision how the beginnings of tea have traveled far and wide, beginning with those of wealth and position and then passed down to the average person. Tea on the *Titanic* was for everyone, but the elegant settings and careful preparations are what still "invite" our attention.

"In nothing more is the English genius for domesticity more notably declared than in the institution of this festival - almost one may call it - of afternoon tea. The mere clink of cups and saucers tunes the mind to happy repose."
George Gissing

Chapter 3
The Pleasures of Tea

Most cruise ships and luxury hotels offer afternoon tea, and depending on the registry of the ship, the tea may be quite authentic. A proper English Afternoon Tea would consist of small crustless tea sandwiches, scones served with jam and Devonshire Clotted Cream, Sweets and Pastries, and the faithful pot of hot tea. The importance of tea during the Victorian and Edwardian era, and the great number of Irish and British passengers and crew on the *Titanic,* made afternoon tea a high priority on that fateful ship.

While many venues will commemorate in countless ways the 100th anniversary of the *Titanic*, preparing and serving an afternoon tea perhaps can best help preserve the legacy of those who sailed on the extraordinary and grand *Titanic*. Creating a *Tea on the Titanic* in your home will let you partake in what many women in the early 1900s experienced when they practiced hospitality. Keep in mind that many of those women had butlers who served the tea, cooks who prepared the tea, and housekeepers who cleaned the house!

Tea was an integral part of the culture of those days, as it still is in England. Increasingly, Americans are regaining an interest and awareness of the soothing social occasion of afternoon tea. Creating a tea for friends and family in your home will give you a delightful sense of pleasure as you practice something that has been a custom for generations. While preparing for tea, you may discover the joy of using your Grandmother's teapot, or drinking tea from your Mother's morning teacup, or using some of the vintage linens hand-embroidered by an auntie.

If this a new venture for you, plan to have fun scouring flea markets and antique shops to find just the right items you need for teatime.

Thousands of pieces of china and silver and such fine dining items, were testimony of the fact that everything to the last detail was done right on the *Titanic*. It was common knowledge that the White Star Line was the "cream of the crop" when it came to passenger accommodations. Unlike many of the ocean liners of that time, the *Titanic* did not require the third-class passenger to bring their own food, dishes, and silverware. Third-class passengers were not accustomed to stopping in the middle of the afternoon for a three-course tea, so a pot of tea and cookies, or biscuits as they are called in England, would have been provided for them in either of two dining rooms located on the F deck. A multi-purpose room, called the General Room, was a place where the steerage passengers could go to read, play cards, visit with other passengers, or perhaps have a cup of tea. Second-class passengers all dined at the same time in a very large, oak-paneled room. The tables were covered with linen tablecloths and the food was served on the White Star china.

Meals for both First- and Second-class passengers were prepared in the same kitchen, with Second-class having three to four courses and First-class as many as eleven! Second-class also had a beautiful library with large windows, large bookcases, and plush carpeting which provided a very cozy atmosphere for afternoon tea. The Veranda Café, the Promenade Café, or Café Parisien, all first-class accommodations, would provide the ideal setting for a lovely afternoon tea. The Veranda Café was separate from the main area of the ship, with large windows, palm trees and ivy, and comfortable wicker furniture - a charming place for a quiet visit and teatime.

The White Star line ordered china from Royal Crown Derby for the A' la Carte Restaurants on both the *Titanic* and her sister ship, the *Olympic*. The style, OSNC (Ocean Steam Navigation Company) had the monogram in green within a wreath on a white background. Royal Crown Derby, established in 1750, was not able to add "Royal" to their name until 1890, when Queen Victoria gave her seal of approval and awarded the royal warrant to the company. A royal warrant is a mark of recognition given to a company that has supplied goods or services for at least five years to the Royal family. It gives the company the right to use the term, "By Appointment," and display the Royal Coat of Arms on their property and products. The reason the A' la Carte Restaurant chose its pattern appears to be simply "more to their liking" according to their own literature. On January 31st, 1911, the order for *Titanic's* china was placed with Royal Crown Derby. The order included:

600 Dinner Plates
150 Soup Plates
150 Breakfast Plates
100 Salad Plates
150 Breakfast Cups & Saucers
100 Teacups & Saucers
36 Creams
25 *Slop Basins

*Slop Basins were bowls used at the tea table to empty the dregs, leaves and grounds from the teacup before fresh tea was poured.

Royal Crown Derby today is reproducing this china to commemorate the *Titanic's* 100-year anniversary. A teapot is priced at $500 and a teacup and saucer for about $225. This would certainly authenticate your *Titanic Tea*! It is believed this is the china pattern used in the afternoon tea service in the First-class salons.

The ship's A' la Carte dining rooms had a remarkable resemblance to those of The Ritz in London; its head chef, Luigi Gatti, was hired from the famous Hotel, and the owner of the Ritz, Cesar Ritz, trained the *Titanic's* restaurant staff. The menus and food for all the dining rooms were far superior on the White Star Lines to other ships of that time.

The staff were not employees of the *Titanic*, but of the head chef. I have had afternoon tea at The Ritz in London and it is still an exceptional event, so there is little doubt, that the afternoon tea on the *Titanic*, supervised by Mr. Gatti, would have been on par with the hotel.

I find that every day, no matter where I am, when it is very close to 4:00 p.m., my internal clock reminds me that it is teatime! No matter the time of year, I need a cup of tea. Not iced tea, not sweet tea, but hot black English tea with milk. Even writing about tea stimulates my desire for that delicious brew. Tea can be taken anywhere, anytime, but don't let me miss my afternoon "cuppa." A spot of tea is always calming. Try it for your afternoon reprieve.

The pleasures of tea is a celebration of friendship, offering comfort to those in your personal circle. There is something about tea that brings out the very essence of hospitality.

The dictionary defines hospitality as the receiving and entertaining of guests, generously and kindly. I believe there is a distinction between entertaining and hospitality. Entertaining connotes being amusing, offering a show or a performance that is interesting and pleasurable. Hospitality, on the other hand, implies offering a guest a place of shelter and healing. Hospitality comes from the root word, hospice, which means the qualities of comfort and care. Entertaining can easily lead to pride and an obsession with perfection. Looking at the glossy magazine covers in the check-out line at the grocery store reinforces this concept. The racks are crowded with magazines on decorating and cooking. Entertaining is big business. Although we can get some wonderful ideas for food preparation and decorating from magazines, the model for hospitality is in the Word of God. "Be hospitable to one another without complaint." 1 Peter 4:9. Entertaining seeks repayment, and usually a return invitation. Each successive affair can take on a form of competition, with each outdoing the previous. But hospitality is a gift to others, the joy of serving and giving, with no thought of repayment. This joy of serving offers our family and friends a peaceful and tranquil atmosphere amid a world of chaos and confusion.

The art of afternoon tea is nothing more than having a plan and then following through. It involves time and work, but oh, will you love the rewards. My mother used to say, "Do what you can, where you are, with what you have." This takes the pressure off your need to perform and allows you to be involved in the joy of making your guests feel at home and sharing a tradition that can be as grand and resplendent as the *Titanic's*.

There are three varieties of the English tea party. The most popular is the *Traditional Afternoon Tea*, which consists of savories, scones with jam and cream, and sweets and desserts. This is usually served between 3:00 p.m. and 5:00 p.m. It is rather formal in nature, protocol and etiquette prevailing. Another tea is the *Cream Tea*. It is less formal and much easier to prepare, as it consists of scones with jam and cream, and a pot of tea, and is also served in the afternoon.

Many believe *High Tea* is a regal and fancy tea, but in reality it is the least elaborate of the three teas. Many tearooms, hotel and cruise ships advertise "high" tea as a posh and elegant tea, but the only thing "high" about this tea is the price. It is the same thing as supper for most of the average folks in England and America.

With a little bit of education in the art of afternoon tea, some planning and preparation, anyone can welcome guests into their home. Whether you live in an apartment, or a castle, your home is a place where you can practice hospitality. I know, as I continue to experiment with new recipes, casual or elegant table settings, new tea blends, in different rooms of my house. Even if things don't flow as smoothly as I would like, the effects always seem to be similar…everyone has a great time.

When I am asked, "Where is your favorite place to have tea?" My response is always the same: "My home." My hope is that you will enjoy giving away your gift of hospitality as we prepare to serve afternoon tea.

"Tea is the ultimate form of hospitality."
Amy Vanderbilt

Chapter 4
Molly Brown on the Titanic

The fateful sinking of the *Titanic* in 1912 launched Margaret Brown to international fame almost overnight. She is nearly as famous as the magnificent ship itself; one rarely talks about one without the other.

A new American millionaire, Margaret "Molly Brown" was among the first-class passengers who boarded the *Titanic* in Cherbourg, France. She was spending the social season in Europe, but was called back to America by the news of her ailing grandson. She wanted to return to her home in Denver as quickly as possible, so booked passage on the first available ship. The *Titanic* was set to sail on April 10th, and Mrs. Brown quickly made arrangements to be on board. She was assigned two cabins in First Class, for a cost of $4,000 -- almost $80,000 in today's economy! Some historians believe that Mrs. Brown had been traveling in Europe with Mr. and Mrs. John Jacob Astor, who were also first-class passengers.

Mrs. Brown was a most remarkable woman. She has been written about, talked about, and immortalized in a Broadway musical, and the 1964 movie starring Debbie Reynolds as the "Unsinkable Molly Brown." She had a reputation as a "mover and a shaker." Margaret Tobin was born to Irish-Catholic immigrant parents in Hannibal, Missouri (Mark Twain's birthplace) in 1867. As a teenager, she helped with the family income by working in a factory. She found the conditions deplorable and wanted to help those trapped in such horrible work places. She dreamed of moving west and making an impact on her community. At the age of eighteen, Margaret and her brother Daniel moved to the mining town of Leadville, Colorado. She worked long and hard hours in a department store, and then started her community service by volunteering in soup kitchens. Not long after the move, she met James Joseph Brown, a mining engineer from Pennsylvania, at a church picnic. J.J., as he was called, was thirteen years older than Margaret. She had planned on marrying for money, but said on many occasions that she "married J.J. for love." They married in 1886 and had two children, Lawrence and Helen.

In 1891, after several years of marriage, the Browns became "overnight millionaires." J.J. had been involved with the Ipex Mining Company in Leadville and with three other business associates developed the Little Jonny Mine. J.J. developed a means of shoring up the walls of the mine, enabling the miners to go deeper. They struck gold, and the Little Jonny Mine became one of the biggest and richest in Colorado. Soon Margaret's dream of investing her money and her time in social concerns became a reality. The Browns moved to Denver in 1894 and bought the house at 1340 Pennsylvania Street for $30,000, an outrageous sum at that time. It remained their family home for almost 50 years. The house at one time served as the Governor's Mansion and in 1970 it became a museum when purchased by Historic Denver, a non-profit organization whose goal has been the restoration of the mansion.

Victorian dining was a wonderful experience for any guest invited to the Brown mansion. The historical organization has restored and furnished the home as it was in the early 1900s. The dining room is resplendent with china teacups and silver pieces that were in use when the Browns entertained. Margaret and her husband became an important part of Denver's social scene. Often wrongly portrayed as being "coarse, uneducated, and loud," Margaret learned five languages, and traveled to Europe to study literature, music, and drama. Sometimes shunned by the social women of Denver, she continued to be known as a flamboyant woman of passion, but was known for her kindness to all. As an employer, she often invited the household help to dine in the family dining room, a practice that offended many of the influential socialites of the time. The Victorians didn't cross social barriers, a custom that Mrs. Brown found ridiculous. She spent one Thanksgiving providing dinner at the Brown Palace Hotel for 1500 street urchins. That didn't fit the social life of many of Denver's elite, either!

A group known as the "Sacred Thirty-Six"- wealthy, conservative Denverites, headed by Mrs. Crawford Hill - did not view the Browns as worthy enough to join their group. The thirty-six (the number of people needed to fill nine bridge tables) did not approve of women being involved in politics, so Margaret was not highly regarded in prestigious social circles. However, the Browns were part of a different, newer, and dauntless social circle that loved Margaret and sought out her energy and expertise to chair many fundraisers and events. Margaret had a great rapport with the press and even when Mrs. Crawford Hill publicly scoffed her in a Denver Post gossip column, Margaret continued with her efforts to help those in need.

Margaret was a women's rights advocate and ran twice unsuccessfully for the U.S. Senate. The juvenile court system was one of her most prized projects. She was very influential in advocating for new laws that separated juveniles from adult inmates. She also spearheaded a campaign to raise funds for the beautiful Catholic Cathedral of Immaculate Conception, which was just a few blocks from their home. The church was an integral part of their family life and the main reason the Browns never divorced. Unfortunately, Margaret and J.J quietly separated in 1909 after 23 years of marriage and remained separated until J.J.'s death in 1922.

Mrs. Brown was one of the lucky ones who survived the sinking of the *Titanic*. She worked tirelessly to get as many women and children into the lifeboats and was finally "pushed" into the lifeboat herself, just as it was being lowered. Each lifeboat had room for 65, but Lifeboat #

6 only carried 24; 21 women, two men and one young boy. Pictures of Lifeboat # 6 with Mrs. Brown and other passengers rowing towards the *Carpathia* are in the upstairs hallway of the Molly Brown House. Molly is said to have been the "captain" of lifeboat # 6 and kept those on board from despair and fear.

When the lifeboat was rescued by the *Carpathia* about 4:30 in the morning, Mrs. Brown refused care for herself, and worked tirelessly helping other survivors get food, warm drinks, and blankets. When the *Carpathia* arrived in New York, the unsinkable Mrs. Brown was in the spotlight for her bravery and her fund raising efforts. More than $10,000 was collected from the *Carpatia's* passengers and crew to help defray medical costs for the survivors. When reporters were permitted to interview those on the *Carpathia*, they asked her to give an account of how she had survived. She replied, "Typical Brown luck, we're unsinkable!" It was this fame and her tenacious attitude that promoted and funded the *Titanic Survivor's Committee* to help the immigrants who survived the *Titanic* disaster. She was instrumental in having a memorial erected in Washington, D.C., to remember the souls lost in the tragic sinking. She was unable to testify in the Congressional inquiry into the sinking of the *Titanic* because she was a woman, but that did not stop her. Just as she had agitated for safety reforms for miners, she petitioned Congress for new regulations for lifeboats and safety aboard all sea going vessels. Many maritime laws are a direct result of her actions.

After Mr. and Mrs. Brown separated, J.J. moved to the American Southwest, as the climate was better for his health. All those years in the mines in Leadville had taken their toll, but the move seemed to be the right thing for him. Margaret leased out the mansion on Pennsylvania Street and moved east to continue her zest for life. She actively pursued an interest in the stage, and lived the life of the new woman of the 1920s; free, liberated, and self-sufficient. At the end of her life, she was living at the Barbizon Hotel for Women. In 1932, she died alone in her sleep at the age of 65, of a brain aneurysm. During an interview earlier in her life, she said, "I found many opportunities in life to be useful, and I was glad to be. The less you think of yourself, the better off you are." She was awarded the French Legion of Honor Award the same year she died for her bravery and being "Unsinkable." Margaret was never known as "Molly" during her lifetime, but that is how she lives in history.

"Accept life daily not as a cup to be drained, but as a chalice to be filled with whatsoever things are honest, pure, lovely and of good report."
Sidney Lovett

Teatime at the Molly Brown House

The Molly Brown House in Denver is home to many teas and special events. My friends and I have taken our granddaughters to many of these teas. They are held on the third-floor of the mansion, always include a tour of the home, and often incorporate programs that bring the Victorian era to life through the narrations of costumed docents who love history. Many of the teas are centered on holidays; some for children, and of course the *Titanic* Teas. Numerous events, dinners, teas, and lectures are planned in 2012 at the Molly Brown House to commemorate the 100-year anniversary.

*For more information on The Molly Brown House, go to: www.MollyBrown.org

Unsinkable Molly Brown Tea

Tea Sandwiches

English Cucumber
Smoked Scottish Salmon
Coronation Chicken
Stilton and Pear

Scones

Queen's Cream Scones
Homemade Lemon Clotted Cream
Strawberry or Raspberry Preserves

Desserts

White Star Cakes
Fruit Tarts
Chocolate Shortbread Bites

Teas

Earl Grey
Black Currant
Darjeeling

Recipes for Unsinkable Molly Brown Tea

English Cucumber Tea Sandwiches

1 English Hothouse Cucumber
Room temperature butter
Thin sliced white bread
Dill

Peel and slice an English hothouse cucumber as thin as possible. Place in a colander and sprinkle with a small amount of white vinegar and salt. Place a plate and large unopened can on top to weigh it down. Leave to drain for at least 30 minutes. Place cucumber on paper towels and press out any remaining liquid. Spread white bread with softened butter and cover with cucumber slices, sprinkle lightly with dill. Top with second slice of buttered bread, trim crusts and cut into four squares, triangles or fingers.

Optional: use cream cheese instead of butter.

Smoked Scottish Salmon Sandwiches

8 slices rye or pumpernickel bread
1/4 cup butter, softened
4 oz smoked salmon slices
2 oz watercress (stems removed)
Pepper and dill weed

Spread butter over slices of bread
Arrange slices of salmon on top of 4 slices of buttered bread
Season with pepper and dill weed
Place watercress on top of salmon slices
Place remainder of bread on top of watercress
Trim crusts from bread and cut into four quarters...triangles or squares

Coronation Chicken Sandwiches

2 cups cooked and chopped chicken
3-4 sticks of celery, chopped
3 oz dried apricots, chopped
1 oz slivered almonds
1/4 jar mango or peach chutney (cut up large bits of fruit)
1 teaspoon curry powder, these vary so adjust to taste
3 chopped green onions
Salt and pepper to taste
Enough mayonnaise to hold salad together

Place all ingredients in bowl and mix well.
Spread on white or whole wheat sandwich slices
Cut off crusts and then cut into desired shapes
This sandwich is usually a favorite, so make plenty.
(Two quarters per person of each sandwich are average)

Stilton and Pear Sandwiches

8 slices Honey Whole Wheat Bread (thin sliced)
1/4 cup softened butter
1 ripe pear, any variety, sliced thin (sprinkled with lemon juice to prevent browning)
4 oz Stilton Cheese, crumbled
Spread butter onto all slices of bread

Place slices of pear on top of 4 slices of bread, overlapping slightly
Divide cheese and place on top of pear slices
Top with other slices of buttered bread
Cut off crusts, and cut into desired shapes.

Queens Tea Scones

2 cups all-purpose flour (plus more for dusting)
1/2 cup sugar
2 teaspoons baking powder
1/4 teaspoon salt
6 tablespoons unsalted butter, cut into 1/2-inch pieces
3/4 cup heavy cream
1 egg, beaten

Glaze:
1 cup powdered sugar
1/2 lemon, juiced

Preheat oven to 375° F. Line a baking sheet with parchment paper. In the bowl of a food processor, pulse together the flour, sugar, baking powder, salt and butter until the mixture resembles a coarse meal. Add the egg and slowly add in the cream until the mixture comes together.

On a lightly floured board, roll out the dough to about 1/2 inch thick. Cut the dough into triangles and put on the prepared baking sheet. Bake for 18 to 20 minutes, or until the edges are golden brown. Transfer the scones onto a wire rack and cool for 30 minutes.

For the glaze: In a medium bowl, mix together the lemon juice and powdered sugar until smooth. Drizzle the glaze over the scones. Makes about 12 scones. Serve with Jam and clotted cream. (People Magazine, Maureen Petrosky)

Homemade Lemon Clotted Cream

3 oz mascarpone cheese
1 cup heavy whipping cream
1/4 teaspoon lemon extract
3 tablespoons powdered sugar
Zest of 1 lemon

In mixing bowl fitted with a whisk, whip the heavy cream until soft peaks, add the remaining ingredients and whip until evenly combined. (People Magazine, Maureen Petrosky)

White Star Cakes

1 package white cake mix
4 oz cream cheese
1/2 cup softened butter
1 1/2 cups powdered sugar
1 tablespoon cocoa and extra for sifting

Spray a jelly-roll pan (or two 9" X 13" pans) with nonstick baking spray, then line with parchment paper.

Prepare cake as directed on package. Pour batter into prepared Jelly-roll pan (or divide batter between the two 9" X 13" pans) and bake for 10 to 15 minutes, or until a wooden toothpick inserted into center comes out clean. Cool on wire rack in pan for about 5 minutes. Then carefully turn out onto a cutting board or counter lined with wax paper. Let cool completely. Cut cake with 2 inch shaped star cookie cutters. In large bowl, combine the cream cheese and the butter until fluffy. Gradually add the powdered sugar and cocoa and beat until smooth. Carefully spread or pipe frosting onto half of the stars, then top with remaining stars. Refrigerate until ready to serve. Sprinkle sifted cocoa on top just before serving. Makes about 12 cakes.

Fruit Tarts

1 box of refrigerated pie crusts (2 crusts) - soften to room temperature

Filling:

1 4-oz box instant lemon pie filling
1 cup cold milk
1 tablespoon grated lemon zest
Whipped cream for topping
1 pint fresh raspberries
Mint leaves for garnish

On a lightly floured surface, unroll pie crusts. Using 3-inch round cutter, cut 14 to 16 circles from dough. Press each dough circle into ungreased muffin tins. Prick the bottom with a fork several times. Bake for 5 to 7 minutes or until golden brown. Cool completely on a wire rack (about 15 minutes).

Mix the milk, lemon zest and pie filling mix with electric mixer or whip until well blended. Spoon pudding mix into cooled tart shells. Top with a dollop of whipped cream, a raspberry and 2 mint leaves.

Chocolate Shortbread Bites

1 cup flour
1/3 cup butter at room temperature
1/4 cup powdered sugar
2 eggs
1 oz unsweetened chocolate, melted in microwave on defrost, cooled
1 cup sugar
1/2 teaspoon baking powder
1/4 teaspoon salt
1 teaspoon vanilla

Combine the flour, butter and powdered sugar until mixed well. Press into an 8-inch square baking dish and bake at 350 degrees for 20 minutes. Beat remaining ingredients together until fluffy. Pour this mixture over the hot cookie crust and bake for another 20 to 25 minutes or until set. Cool and cut into squares. Can be made ahead and kept in an airtight container. Makes 16.

"There are two ways of spreading light - to be the candle or the mirror that reflects it."
Edith Wharton

Tea

Chapter 5
The Essentials of Afternoon Tea

I have often wondered what it would be like to have afternoon tea on the *Titanic.* The Royal Crown China, the gleaming silver tea trays filled with delectable treats, the soothing cup of tea, and the efficient wait staff, making sure everything was ship-shape. It would have been a memorable event.

Last year our family traveled on the Celebrity Millennium cruise ship, which has a nostalgic, specialty dining room called *The Olympic*. Passengers are given the opportunity to experience turn-of-the century dining elegance of the great ocean liners.

This restaurant is resplendent with dark walnut panels that once adorned the first-class, a la carte dining room of the *RMS Olympic*, sister ship of the *Titanic* and *Britannic.* Woodworkers and craftsmen from as far away as Palestine were brought to Ireland at the beginning of the 20th century to carve and gild the rich paneling.

When the *RMS Olympic* was dismantled for scrap in 1935, the paneling was bought and installed in a private home in Southport, England. The house was later sold in the 1990s to Celebrity Cruise Lines and the paneling installed in *The Olympic* restaurant aboard the Millennium. Original china from the White Star's *Olympic*, a 55-pound brass dinner bell, a large chandelier from the *Olympic's* first-class lounge, and two bottles of rare uncorked champagne, are part of the vintage items that contribute to this dining experience's authenticity. To see so many items that probably duplicate things on the *Titanic* is thrilling. The sister ships were almost identical and there are rumors that the *Titanic* might have been switched with the *Olympic* at the last minute, and it was the *Olympic* that sunk, not the *Titanic.* These rumors remain a mystery.

During our cruise, *The Olympic* offered passengers a Champagne Afternoon Tea. Six of our family members attended. The service was excellent, as all of the waiters were also *chefs du rang,* very knowledgeable of the menu and preparation. The elegant food selection for our tea was presented on three-tiered silver plate-stands. The traditional scones were on top; then sandwiches; and on the lowest plate, delightful sweets and desserts. Devonshire cream, jam, and lemon curd for our scones, were served in dainty little china bowls. The wonderful variety of sandwiches was replenished frequently. We had many choices for tea: the traditional English breakfast; Darjeeling; Assam; numerous decaf selections; and a favorite of mine, Lapsong Souchong, a smoky black tea.

Many people think that afternoon tea is just for ladies, but the two young men sharing tea with us seemed to enjoy the event immensely, and did not admit to feeling hungry when we left. Half of the Afternoon Tea party were gentlemen. The custom has been perfectly described by cruise-ship expert and author of "The Only Way to Cross," John Maxtone-Graham: "fine dining and an ocean view at the same time."

Despite not sailing on the *Titanic*, we had a legitimate glimpse of having afternoon tea on that grand ship. We were able to relax in the elegant and comfortable furnishings of a stunning room, surrounded by vintage décor, and treated as first-class passengers. We enjoyed the benefits of a time-honored ritual in a bygone era of elegance, while enjoying life aboard a modern cruise ship with all the amenities. It was the perfect pairing of old and new.

The traditional English Afternoon Tea ceremony uses many items from former years that might not be part of your own kitchen utensils and gadgets. The correct word for "tea-stuff" is accoutrements - items used for particular activities and functions. Following is a list of commonly needed accoutrements for giving a tea:

- Tea Kettle – preferably electric
- Teapot
- Tea Strainer, Tea Ball or Infuser
- Teacups and saucers
- Small Tea Plates
- Teaspoons
- Tea or fruit knives
- Dessert Forks
- Tea: Loose or teabags
- Sugar Bowl
- Sugar Tongs and sugar cubes
- Milk Jug (creamer)
- Serving Plates and Dishes
- Tablecloth
- Serviettes (tea napkins 12")
- Serving Tray and Cloth
- Tea Cozy
- Nice Extras: Flowers, Candles, Music, Place Cards and Favors

After looking at this list, you might realize that you already own many of the items. Don't overlook your china service, as most have teacups and saucers and dessert plates; and some include teapots. I encourage you to use items already in your home, and then add accoutrements as you are able.

The most important accoutrement needed for an afternoon tea is a teapot. The function of any teapot is to brew and dispense tea. There is an abundant variety of teapots. Some are very elegant, made of fine bone china or silver; others are simple designs made of stoneware, pottery, clear glass, or stainless steel. There are certain shapes and styles that will appeal to you because of color or pattern. The most popular shape is the rounded belly. Unfortunately, not all teapots are designed to make and pour tea. Some teapots are purely art objects. They are beautiful but would be totally impractical for serving tea.

Do not confuse teapots with teakettles. Kettles are placed on the stove to boil the water. The teapot is never placed on a burner. Electric kettles are by far the most useful of any of the accoutrements… and are easy to find in any department or discount store. Yes, afternoon tea is a merging of the old and new!

When you buy a teapot, whether it's your first or an addition to your collection, pick it up by the handle and see how it feels in your hand. Your hand and fingers should have room to avoid being burned by the hot teapot. The lid should have a lug or little lip, positioned to the back of the teapot, to keep it from falling off during pouring, and should also have a tiny hole to allow air into the pot when pouring. This will help the pot to minimize dripping when pouring the tea. Ask the salesperson if it is possible to put water into the teapot to see if it pours properly. Many teapots drip a little; they shouldn't, but some just do, regardless of the design. The design of the spout will sometimes enable the teapot to drip, regardless of its placement on the pot. The most important advice about buying a teapot is – buy one you love!

If you shop for a used teapot, run your finger around the edge and hold the teapot up to light, in order to see any chips or cracks. Also, a chip on the bottom of the spout will most often cause the teapot to drip when pouring. When buying antique teapots, it is important to check for cracks and leaks. This is one time you *need* to put water into it before buying, unless you will only be using it for decorative purposes. Check that the handle has not been broken and repaired, as nothing is worse than having the handle break off when pouring hot, steaming tea! The same advice is good to follow when buying used or antique teacups…check for breaks and chips.

I have several Chatsford teapots. They are made in England and come with a great, nylon mesh infusion basket, which allows the tea-leaf room for expansion, and is quick and easy to clean. I also have bought the smaller infusion baskets to use with my smaller teapots.

If you want to clean your teapot to rid it of the build up of tea, a good remedy is baking soda. A tablespoon into the pot, then pour in boiling water, and let it sit for about 30 minutes. Others have told me that denture-cleaning tablets work well, but I would avoid using bleach. When storing teapots after washing and drying, I place a sugar cube in each one, to absorb any leftover moisture, and to keep the pot smelling sweet.

I think teapots have a personality of their own. There is adventure in searches for the perfect teapot...and like any collector, it's fun to hunt and a joy to make discoveries. Each teapot in my collection has a story. Some were gifts, others I bought at estate sales, antique shops, or garage sales, and some were passed on to me when my mother died. Check the bottom of the teapot for the markings of the manufacturer and country of origin, and that will add more interest to each one you buy. Then, if possible, try to use them all: I frequently rotate their positions on my shelves. Once your family and friends discover you are becoming a teapot or teacup collector, their shopping for gifts is easy. I cannot tell you how many times I receive tea gifts, and rarely are they duplicates.

One young woman in California wanted to have teas in her home to reach out to her neighbors, but only had a couple of teacups. I suggested going out early Saturday mornings and scouring garage sales. Several weeks later, she called and shared her exciting story. She had finally found a lovely bone china teacup from England. When she asked the lady having the sale if she had more, the lady took her inside her home and sold her six more cups and saucers and the shelf that held them – all for thirty dollars. That friend has been having her neighbors and friends to tea ever since, and now her daughters are sharing their love of tea with their teen friends.

Choosing the Tea:

During the early 1900s, choices for tea were limited. Afternoon tea on the *Titanic* would have had few choices: black; oolong; Earl Grey; and Darjeeling.

Steerage passengers probably had one tea, black. That all might have been a blessing, as the incredible varieties of tea today can be overwhelming!

Because tea is such an international beverage, you can find some very good teas at your neighborhood food store or the numerous tea web sites. I have mentioned that loose-leaf tea will give you a better tasting tea and more choices than teabags; also, loose tea has a much smaller environmental footprint! Every teabag requires paper or nylon mesh, a staple, string, and a paper tag. That may seem rather insignificant, but multiply that by the billions of teabags used annually; loose tea is a less expensive option and it tastes better!

Thanks to the increasing popularity of tea, there are more places to enjoy tea. However, I believe the tea experience is more pleasant and less expensive, when you savor the experience in your own home. It gives you the opportunity to experiment with a much larger choice of teas… and you are able to share your gift of hospitality!

- Black tea is the number-one seller, and continues to offer many variations that would include: Kenya, Assam, Keemun, Darjeeling, English and Irish Breakfast, Chai, Earl Grey, and Lapsong Souchong.
- Oolong teas are the ones usually served in Asian restaurants. These teas are not as oxidized as Black tea, and have a lovely amber color. Many oolongs are mixed with flavors, and can be a wonderful choice for an afternoon drink.
- Green Tea has for several years been gaining in popularity… mainly because studies showed it had more antioxidants and had healthier properties than black tea, but that theory has

proven false. There was also a falsehood that green tea had less caffeine. Nevertheless, green tea is very popular and here to stay. Many green teas are flavored with the same fruits and spices found in flavored black teas.

- Flavored Black Tea Blends include black currant, strawberry, lemon, orange spice, vanilla… the sky is the limit.
- White Tea is light-toned, with a softer and subtler taste. The same flavors are available in white teas as the others. The cost of this tea is higher because of infrequent harvesting.
- Tisanes – herbal infusions that contain no tea. Examples are rooibos, mint, chamomile, matè, and hibiscus.

The Perfect Pot of Tea:

Brewing the perfect pot of tea is a very personal art. Every aspect is determined by several factors: the quality of tea used; the temperature of the water; and the age of the teapot. Seasoned teapots make a great cup of tea and they get that way by continued use.

Always use fresh cold water to make tea, as there is a higher content of oxygen in fresh water. The oxygen helps release the oils and flavors in tea and provides better tasting tea. While the water is boiling in your teakettle, fill the teapot with hot tap water to prepare and warm the teapot. Remove the hot water from the teapot once the water in the tea kettle has come to a boil. Measure the tea leaves and place them directly into the pot, or into an infuser or tea ball. Pour the boiling water over the tea leaves, replace the lid and steep for three to five minutes for black teas. White, green and oolong teas need the water to be just short of boiling and require a steep time of two to three minutes.

Do not leave tea leaves in the water longer than the recommended steeping time, as the tea will become bitter. Leaving them longer does not make the tea stronger. Placing a tea cozy over the teapot will keep your tea hot for about 30 minutes or longer.

If you are using teabags, the same instructions apply. The boiling water is always poured over the tea; the teabag is not dunked into the water.

Rarely will I order tea in a restaurant, for several reasons. The water is usually lukewarm, not boiling; and the teabags often are inexpensive and of poor quality. I won't mention names, but if you do use teabags, buy the best quality you can find.

A friend of mine was very excited about entertaining her husband's grandmother who was coming for a visit from England. This was to be their first meeting, and she wanted everything to be just right. Of course, she would serve her tea, and had her best mugs ready. She brought in the mug with the teabag tag, a well-known brand I might add, hanging over the cup's edge, and presented it to the grandmother. Imagine her surprise when the spry little lady jumped up, grabbed her grandson's wife by the hand and marched her out to the kitchen. With great flourish she tossed the tea, teabag and all, into the sink. "Now, let's learn how to make a proper cup of tea, my dear." With that, she promptly pulled out a tin of tea and tea strainer from her handbag and proceeded to prepare a proper pot of tea!

The basic rules for making great tea have not changed for thousands of years. Follow the directions and you will make the perfect pot of tea. Experiment with different types of teas, mix teas, and take time to enjoy the perfect cup of tea.

"Better to be deprived of food for three days,
than tea for one."
Ancient Chinese Proverb

Chapter 6
The Art of Afternoon Tea

Growing up in an English home on the plains of South Dakota was a unique experience for me. My mother and I were born in England and came to America after World War II. Tea was part of everyday life in our family, and my mother, who had a gracious gift of hospitality, taught me to prepare and serve Afternoon Tea. She encouraged me by example to use my home for the comfort of others by providing the example and opportunity to be hospitable.

I have tried to follow in her footsteps, and have even converted many of my coffee-drinking friends to tea lovers. When we gather, we sense a change in the atmosphere as we settle down to enjoy a cup of tea. There is a serenity not found in restaurants or coffee shops. Celebrating teatime is a wonderful way to practice hospitality in our homes.

With our busy lifestyles, an afternoon tea has many advantages. Most of the food can be prepared before the guests arrive. The tea needs to be made only as you begin serving the food. I try to do as much as possible the few days before the tea. Ideally, plan on getting a little time to rest before everyone arrives, so you can enjoy the fruits of your labor. It is much better to serve less food than be tired when your guests arrive. The pleasure and comfort of your friends is the top priority. It isn't so much what we put on the table to serve, but whom we are serving in the chairs!

Planning is the key. You may be a spontaneous person who does everything on a "wing and a prayer," but the majority of us need a blueprint to keep things in order, especially having guests for afternoon tea. Start a list and keep track of your progress. Don't forget to delegate. Husbands and children can make a big difference in getting things done.

A successful tea will have everything ready and organized before the guests arrive. Work backward with your time planner; then you will be able to gauge if you have time to make that extra dessert. Start a tea party journal. Jot down the date, guests, menu, and any other little tidbits to help you remember the event. It makes planning your next tea easier.

Keys to a Successful Tea:

- Set the date and time for your tea.
- Make a guest list and send out the invitations at least two weeks in advance if possible. (No e-mails!)
- Plan the menu and the shopping list.
- Check your linens, serving dishes, silver, etc.
- Prepare as much of the food as possible in advance.
- Set the table the day before.

Creating a tea with my mother was always a breeze, as she was a natural-born organizer. I tend to "wing it," so the first tea I planned on my own was overwhelming. My friend Carol and I decided to have a bridal tea instead of a luncheon. Both of us were "experts" in giving dinner parties and luncheons, so how hard could a tea be? We found out! Having 43 ladies for afternoon tea is not easy. However, the rewards of our planning paid off when most of the women, who had never been to a tea, wanted to know when we could have a tea party again. That was many years ago, but neither of us put the teacups away. My advice is to start with a smaller amount of guests. I once read that six guests "are a more confidence-inspiring number to serve," and I agree.

There are three different types of tea parties:

1. *The Traditional Afternoon Tea* - elegant and formal, consisting of three courses served mid-afternoon. Small, crustless tea sandwiches are the first course, then scones with jam and Devonshire cream, and the grand finale: tea cakes; tarts; and cookies.
2. *A Cream Tea* – easy to prepare, but still rather elegant. This tea consists of scones with jam and Devonshire cream, and a pot of tea.
3. *High Tea* – this tea is the traditional evening meal, served after 5:00. This tea is not elaborate, but rather a hearty meal including some substantial meat dish. This tea will be covered in a later chapter, with ideas and recipes.

The Traditional Afternoon Tea is the most popular of the three, and is the one selected for social occasions, such as the first- and second-class tea on the *Titanic*, and in most hotels, restaurants, and tearooms. Oftentimes afternoon tea is advertised as "high" tea, which is incorrect, and one of my pet peeves!

Guests

Once you have decided on the type of tea party you will host, its time will be mandated by tradition, Afternoon and Cream Teas around two or three o'clock and High Tea after five o'clock, so decide on the guest list, and prepare the invitations. Remember, if this is your first attempt to host an afternoon tea, keep the guest list to six guests. Once you have practiced on them, you will know how many to invite for your next party! We tend to invite those friends with whom we have things in common, as conversations are easier and we know what to expect. But real hospitality reaches out to others, especially those who might be lonely or discouraged, or someone who could use a friend. I try to include one person who is outside my circle of acquaintances, to keep my guest list interesting.

Invitations

If you like to make cards, this will be fun for you to do, and your guests will be delighted to receive such an invitation. Attractive little note cards with a tea-motif are readily available, and should be hand-written. Some of the nicest invitations I have seen are cutouts of teapots or teacups with stickers. For a *Titanic Tea*, hand written invitations on a white star (White Star Lines) cutout, or a life preserver made from blue and white construction paper would be perfect. These personal invitations will create anticipation for your *Titanic Tea*. If you need to make phone calls because of lack of time, it is considered acceptable, but e-mail is not proper for a formal engagement. There are many "Evite" web sites, but the respected etiquette for this kind of event should be hand-written invitations.

Key information needed on each invitation:

- Name and purpose of the event
- Day and date
- Time – preferably written in the form of "two o'clock," not "2:00"
- Location
- Appropriate attire or any other instructions
- RSVP with a deadline

Planning your Event

Now, where do we begin? Having a tea party does not have to break the bank or break your back. In fact, afternoon teas are one of the least expensive events to host, and if you spend time to make a plan and follow the plan, you will be a successful hostess. There is no greater joy than having your family or friends around a table and enjoy the sharing of a meal and friendship.

Sandwiches, Scones and Desserts

If you are just starting out, keep it simple. Remember the old saying, "Food should feed the eyes first" - meaning, if it looks good, half the battle is won. As stated earlier, most of the meal can be prepared before your guests arrive. Many items for your tea can be bought prepared, then placed on serving platters. You can add your own personal signature to the dish, such as doilies, flowers, parsley, frosted grapes, fruit slices or leaves. Since you are serving six guests, the food will be served to the guests at the table. With larger numbers of guests, a buffet is the popular serving choice.

For our preparations we are serving the Traditional Afternoon Tea with three courses. A cream tea would follow the same protocol with but one course. The three courses are served and presented in the following sequence: first, the tea sandwiches; second, scones; last the sweets and desserts. The three-tiered plate stands should have scones at the top, as a dome was used in earlier times to keep them warm, but they would still be the second course. Sandwiches should be on the middle tier, and sweets and pastries on the bottom plate.

Select three or four different tea sandwiches to serve at your tea. One should be the traditional cucumber sandwich. Plan on six small quarter sandwiches for each person. If you are serving three different types of sandwiches for a party of six, three slices of bread per person, requires a total of 18 slices. Most loaves of bread have 20 - 22 slices per loaf. It is nice to vary the bread, using some white and some whole wheat, raisin, etc. Depending on which bread you buy, you will have leftovers. Bread freezes well if double wrapped, or placed in a plastic freezer bag. You will have enough bread for your next tea.

Choose the fillings for your sandwiches. Look through the next chapter and choose three or four. Specialty food stores and deli counters have numerous fillings already made, for your consideration. Because it is easier to make sandwiches with frozen bread, place the bread in your freezer upon returning home from the grocery store.

Next, decide which scone or scones you would like to serve. I serve a plain and a fruit scone at each tea. For a cream tea, you might want to have three kinds, made smaller. Scones originated in Scotland in the mid-1600s. The Scots pronounce them "scoon" and the Brits "skon" with a long "o." The etiquette of eating a scone differs from region to region in England. Some prefer to slice it in half then place the jam on first, then top it with clotted cream. Others say the proper way is cream first, then the jam. But both agree that the halves are never put together; each half is eaten separately. Then there are those who break off a small piece and place jam and cream on each bite as it is eaten, which makes eating a scone much easier and not so messy.

"Tea with friends is like clotted cream and jam on scones -- delicious and sweet."
Bobette Barfod

A friend gave a tea for a large group of ladies at her home. She had baked the scones at the last minute. Somewhere she had read - that scones should be made just before serving. The scones did not turn out very well, and another batch was started, just as all the guests were arriving. My friend was up to her elbows in flour and dough. That tea party started late, and needless to say, my friend did not enjoy the afternoon. This situation should be avoided by making the scones before the tea, then heating them on a cookie sheet for a few minutes before serving. I volunteered to make scones for a large Christmas event and made scones every night for about three weeks – 700 scones! These were frozen after baking, and on the night of the event were warmed in large ovens and enjoyed by all. Friends and neighbors were kind enough to let me use their freezers, but that definitely was a time when making the scones in advance was smart.

I like to cook more than I like to bake, so for me, I supplement the table with cakes and such from my local bakery, bought a day before the tea and refrigerated. Delightful fruit tarts and petit fours are the bakery's specialties; they also have wonderful scones, but rarely do I purchase them, as I do like to bake scones myself. The recipes in the next chapter will give you numerous choices.

This part of the planning helps you make a complete grocery list. Anything that will "keep" or freeze, you will want to purchase as early as possible. A couple days before the tea, you will finish your list and buy the perishable items.

Setting the Table

Serving an afternoon tea can take place in several areas of your home, but most often in the dining room. You can also have tea in your living room and use the coffee table for the food and tea service. The kitchen can be transformed into a delightful tearoom if you don't have a dining room. During the winter months, you could serve tea around the coziness of a fire, and in the summer the cool breezes of a porch are very inviting. Whatever room you choose, make it a special place that reflects warmth and graciousness, and tells your guests they are welcome. This is always the main goal of hospitality.

Linens

Tablecloths and serviettes (napkins) for a tea should always be cloth. Remember, we are planning a *Titanic Tea,* and want the tea experience to be like it was during that era. Whichever room you choose for tea, a tablecloth is a necessity for your table. Tea napkins are twelve inches square and can match or coordinate with the tablecloth. There are several options for presenting the napkin on the table: folded and placed across the plate with the knife sitting on top at an angle; in napkin rings; or folded and placed under the fork on your left. Napkins are interesting items as they have been around for centuries and some of their first uses were as bibs. It probably protected the lace and frills worn by both men and women. Today the role of a napkin is much the same, to protect our clothing, but they are also a big part of the tablescape. When leaving the table during the tea, or at the conclusion of the meal, your napkin should be folded and placed on the left side of your place setting, not on the chair.

Napkin Rings

Napkin rings today are purely decorative and can be bought in any home-goods store. I use napkin rings at my teas and like the finished look they add to the table. My daughter has given me several sets of tea-related napkin rings and I always find the ladies love them! Years ago, if guests were asked to place their napkins back into the napkin rings, it was an indication they would be invited back for another visit. That custom is no longer in vogue today. The napkin ring is placed to the left of the guest's plate and remains there until the end of the meal. Many hotels and tearooms don't use napkin rings, but instead fold napkins into intricate shapes to resemble fans, shells, flowers, or hats. Directions for these can be found in napkin-folding books or on the Internet. Lacing a ribbon that matches your décor around the folded napkin and placing a flower under the ribbon makes a quick and easy virtual napkin ring. If you do not use a napkin ring, place the napkin to the left of the plate.

Centerpieces

The top of a centerpiece should be a height that allows guests to see one another. My favorite flowers for centerpieces are roses and greenery placed in teapots. I use teapots as vases when they are cracked or have lost their lids, and are not usable for pouring tea. If the teapot leaks, place a glass inside to hold the water. A doily, either paper or crocheted, can be placed under the teapot, to give a lacey look to the table. A crystal bowl filled with several large peony blooms is a beautiful centerpiece of the correct height. Look for unusual containers in your home that might double as a flower vase and create interest in your table. If you have a flower garden with cutting flowers, your tea table will be the envy of those of us with a "brown" thumb.

Silver Accoutrements

Silverware, silver trays and silver teapots should be polished and gleaming to have center stage on your tea table. I love the charm and elegance that silver adds to the tea setting. Silver was prevalent during the Victorian and Edwardian era, but with the invention of silver-plate and stainless steel, silver polishing seemed to become a dreaded chore. That resulted in silver tea accoutrements becoming more of collector's items. Many antique stores and flea markets are excellent places to find silver pieces for your tea collection. Look for tea strainers in all shapes and sizes, serving spoons, dessert forks, moat spoons, teaspoons, sugar tongs, trays, teapots, and creamer and sugar bowls. My mother had a set of silver "apostle" spoons that I have used for many years. They are smaller than a teaspoon and are always the center of attention, as they are so unique.

Apostle spoons are a set of thirteen spoons, usually silver, with adorned handles, representing Jesus and the twelve apostles. These spoons were originally produced in the 1500s, individually made, and given by wealthy persons to their grandchildren or godchildren as a Christening present. Only that person would then use the spoon, and it would be kept for life. Reproductions, like I have, were much smaller, and were popular wedding gifts in a set of six, with a matching sugar tong. I have collected several sets and use them at every tea.

The Tea Table

An attractive table setting is only one part of the atmosphere you are creating, but it can be the most captivating part of the whole scene. Collecting bone china teacups has been a passion most of my life. Looking at all the teacups I have collected over the many years brings me much pleasure and comfort. A tea table with an eclectic array of cups is more interesting than a matching set, and always a conversation-starter.

The tradition of tea has always linked its history to that of charm and elegance. Nowhere is that more obvious than in the lovely patterns of chintz or floral-appointed bone china. Whether you have matched china sets, such as the *Titanic's* Royal Crown Derby, or you are blending teacups and plates from several patterns, plan ahead before setting the table. Color unifies the table and compliments the food served. The table is comparable to a stage. All the accoutrements are the players. The outcome begins with the backdrop. Since most china has a pattern, solid-colored cloths are the best choice. Napkins and flowers should be coordinated, and tie everything together.

Set the table the night before your tea. Get creative and be original. It's nice to have varied heights in your serving pieces. Many stores now carry cake plate holders as regular stock. There is no right or wrong way to combine china. If you are using your china place settings, layer the plates for a more elegant look. If you are just starting out, use the best you have for this kind of event. Then add to it as time and money permits. I mentioned earlier that a teapot was the first item you should acquire for your tea. Next come teacups, plates, and then the silver pieces (however, having said that, you might find a great buy on a few teacups, or a silver tea strainer... so go for it!) Something that many women do if they do not have enough teacups, is have each guest bring her favorite teacup and then tell why it is special to her.

I have now collected plates to go with most of my teacups. I love to find a trio set, which is the matching teacup, saucer, and tea plate. Before

I had these, I would use a plate that didn't match, and place a paper doily on the plate and cover it with a clear glass plate from the dollar store. This has worked for many women as they continue to collect. If you have a china dinner set, then use it, as it sets a beautiful table.

One last word on setting the table, please try to allow 24 inches for each guest's setting.

Place Cards

I think place cards are one of the little details that make teatime so charming. I like to use the tent style card and then write the guest's name in calligraphy. Dainty porcelain place cards are also another fun purchase, as they are reusable and can double as a marker for foods in a buffet setting. Place cards are for the hostess's benefit as much as the guest's. The guest knows where to sit, and is placed next to someone with whom they might have common interests. A quiet person seated next to someone more outgoing will foster conversation. A place card in the shape of a white star or a life preserver for your *Titanic Tea* will continue the theme.

Tea Etiquette

"Manners are a sensitive awareness of the feelings of others. If you have that awareness, you have good manners, no matter what fork you use." —Emily Post

In reality, etiquette and good manners help others feel comfortable. With the addition of social networking to our society, we are faced with needing new information on correct etiquette. For many years I have taught "The Art of Afternoon Tea" in colleges, churches, private events, and children's parties. At the beginning of each class, at least one person sticks a pinkie finger up in the air, and asks if we will be drinking tea. This is always an indication of limited knowledge of tea;

and at that point, I knew we would be enjoying "Tea 101" again!

We really can't have two sets of manners, one for home and one for the show, but sadly that is the norm and not the exception. Two families were dining in an upscale restaurant. One of the mothers excused herself from the table and the little boy from the other family asked where was she going. His mother replied, "She is going to powder her nose." Later when his mother excused herself from the table, the little boy called after her in a loud voice heard by all the other diners, "Mummy, are you going to polish your bum?" We might find that humorous, but I believe that mother was mortified. It's good to start practicing table manners and etiquette when the children are little!

Having to listen to others' conversations while they talk on cell phones is becoming habitual and annoying. I am pleased to see many business establishments have a sign in the entrance: "No Cell Phones, Please." This is also proper etiquette for afternoon teas. Purses, glasses, keys, lipstick, and cell phones should never be placed on the table. Place them under your chair or better yet, leave them with your coat. This is one problem they did not have on the *Titanic*. In fact, it was the lack of phone coverage that was the greater misfortune.

Tea etiquette is not so different from normal etiquette. A few things to keep in mind will help everyone at the table enjoy each other.

- Since many women love to dress for tea, they will arrive in gloves and hats. Gloves must always be removed for eating. Hats may remain in place if a veil is not covering the face.
- When sitting 12 inches or less from a table, only the teacup is lifted and the saucer is left on the table. If sitting in a living room and using a coffee table, the saucer and cup are lifted together from the table. The left hand holds the saucer and the right hand holds the cup while drinking the tea.
- While drinking tea from the cup, don't look into the cup, but at those around you.

- When stirring the sugar or milk into your tea, never clink the side of your cup with the spoon, but carefully rotate the spoon in a gentle roll several times.
- Always use the sugar tongs, never your finger, to pick up a sugar cube.
- Teacups and saucers should be placed at the 2 o'clock position relative to the plate. The handles of the cups should always be at a right angle and pointed to 4 o'clock with the teaspoon at a right angle behind the cup. This will make your tea table look very proper and organized.
- When not in use, the teaspoon should remain on the saucer, behind the teacup.
- Always use milk when called for, never half-and-half, cream, or cream-substitute coffee flavorings. Whole milk gives the tea a rich flavor, while non-fat can give it a chalky look. Ninety-eight per cent of all Brits take their tea with milk. (Per the U.K. Tea Council).
- Lemons should be in small wedges and served with a fork. It is best to remove the lemon wedges before drinking the tea. If using lemon, do not add milk or it will curdle.
- Are you a Miffy or a Tiffy? A Miffy (milk in first) puts the milk into the cup before pouring the tea, and a Tiffy (tea in first) pours the tea into the cup then adds the milk. Mr. Samuel H. G. Twining, ninth-generation director of Twinings Tea, gave a tea presentation at the Bath Spa Hotel in Bath, England, attended by my cousin, Angela. His advise was contrary to many tea "experts" who insist the tea is poured first. Mr. Twining stated it is correct is to add the milk first! However, the U.K. Tea Council suggests you add the milk after the tea! I have a special affinity with Twinings, as they supplied all the tea for the Red Cross prisoner-of-war parcels, for the Women's Voluntary Service, and for many YMCA wartime canteens,

which my mother was very involved during WW II.

- Serving tea: You, as the hostess, should pour everyone's tea. Never pass the teapot around the table. In Victorian times, this was considered being the "Mum." However, if you have eight or more guests for tea, it is a great honor to ask a dear friend if she would help pour the tea.
- When pouring tea for your guests, make sure the teacup and saucer are sitting on the table, not held up in the air. You will avoid burning someone if you follow this tip.
- Never fill the teacup to the rim. It could easily spill over into the saucer and cause the teacup to drip while drinking.

Etiquette is a customary code of polite behavior in society. It is showing good taste, kindness, and consideration to others. In our world of casual and lackadaisical living, almost anything goes. This is all the more reason for taking the time to prepare and serve others with the traditional refinements of culture and respect. Etiquette will always be the model for good living. This has not changed and will never change.

While we don't have the strict confinements that were in vogue during the *Titanic* years, we have a legacy of politeness and tradition that carries into all areas of life. We must thank those from the earlier generations who left us guidelines for dining etiquette and consideration for others.

"Everything is permissible for me, but not everything is beneficial."
I Corinthians 6:2 NIV

Tea Party Planning Check List

Two Weeks Before

- Set the date and time
- Decide on a theme –*Titanic Tea*
- Determine guest list
- Make or buy invitations
- Mail invitations
- Plan a menu
- Determine a budget

One Week Before

- Check Table Linens and Napkins
- Shop for food items
- Prepare any menu items that can be made ahead and frozen
- Buy or make party favors
- Wash Serving pieces, glassware and silverware
- Polish Silver if necessary
- Follow up with guests who have not RSVP'd
- Create Place cards

Two Days Before

- Buy additional food items
- Write Place cards and determine seating arrangement
- Pick up and arrange flowers
- Plan any music you wish to play

Day Before

- Prepare Sandwich fillings
- Bake scones
- Prepare Desserts
- Set Table and arrange place cards and favors

Morning of

- Finish preparing all food
- Check guest bathroom, set out clean towels
- Bake scones if not done day before
- Have kitchen clean with new trash bag and dishwasher empty

Two hours before

- Put your feet up and have a cup of tea

One hour before

- Get Dressed
- Fill teakettles with fresh water
- Place scones on cookie sheet and cover with foil

Enjoy!

"There are few hours in life more agreeable than the hour dedicated to the ceremony known as afternoon tea."
Henry James

Chapter 7
A Titanic Tea

"Welcome Aboard"

Welcome to *Tea on the Titanic*! Blending the traditions of an English Afternoon Tea from the Edwardian era with the convenience of today's food preparation. This is the tea where we pull out all the stops…the best linen tablecloth and napkins…polished silver… and the table set. Come on board for a Tea-riffic time…we will have the opportunity to prepare not just a *Titanic Tea* but also an *Olympic Tea.*

"Since a restaurant cannot totally rely on its ambiance, the food and service must be impeccable!"

1st Class Afternoon Titanic Tea

Tea Sandwiches

Tarragon and Chicken
Egg and Capers
RMS Salmon
White Star Cucumber

Scones

Ritz Scones
Lemon Poppy Seed Scones
Devonshire cream and jam

Desserts

White Star Chocolate Raspberrry-Cakes

Victoria Sponge Cake

Scottish Shortbread

Teas

Titanic Tea (Special Blend Earl Grey)

Assam

Darjeeling

Recipes for a Titanic Tea

1st Course ~ Sandwiches

Tarragon and Chicken

4 chicken breasts, cooked and chopped or 1 large can of chicken
2/3 cup chopped celery
1 small shallot, finely chopped
1/2 cup dried cranberries
1/2 cup chopped toasted pecans
1 tablespoon finely chopped fresh tarragon leaves
1/2 cup sour cream
Salt and pepper to taste

Combine chicken with all the ingredients and add salt and pepper. Chill for 1 to 2 hours or overnight. Butter white sandwich bread, divide chicken mixture equally on half the bread, and top with the remaining slices. Trim the crusts and cut into desired shape.

Egg and Capers

6 hard boiled eggs, peeled

Place eggs into a bowl and pour cooled, strong Earl Grey Tea over the eggs to cover

Let sit overnight in the refrigerator.

Drain and dry eggs, then mash into fine pieces.

Add enough mayonnaise to moisten so that egg mixture is spreadable.

Add 2 tablespoons drained capers and mix well.

Butter pumpernickel bread, place egg mixture on half the slices, top with remaining bread and trim crusts. Cut into round circles with metal cookie cutter.

RMS Salmon

8 ounces canned salmon, flaked
1/4 cup chopped pecans
1 teaspoon chopped chives
1/4 cup mayonnaise
Wheat Sandwich Bread

Mix salmon and loose ingredients well in medium bowl. Spread bread with softened butter; then spread half of the slices with the salmon mixture, top with other half of the bread slices. Trim the crusts and cut with a star cookie cutter. Lightly spread sides of sandwiches with butter, and roll the sides in finely chopped chives or parsley.

White Star Cucumber

1 English Hot House Cucumber
Softened Butter or Cream Cheese
White and Wheat Sandwich bread
Wash cucumber, but do not peel.

Using a vegetable peeler, peel long strips of cucumber and place on paper towels.

Sprinkle with a little salt, this will help draw out some of the liquid.

Spread butter or cream cheese on each slice of bread; then lay the cucumber strips across the bread, slightly overlapping. Either cut into triangles with sharp knife, or use cookie cutter to make shapes like circles, stars or hearts. Sprinkle a little black pepper and a very small amount of sea salt over the tops of the cucumber and garnish with mint, parsley, cilantro, watercress, or mini violets.

These are very impressive little sandwiches and just the thing for a special tea.

2nd Course ~ Scones

Ritz Scones

1/4 cup butter, softened
1 cup powdered sugar
4 cups pastry flour
2 tablespoons baking powder
1 egg
1 1/4 cups milk
Pinch salt
1/4 cup dried apricots, chopped
1/4 cup raisins

Cream together butter and sugar, then add the pastry flour, baking powder, egg, milk, and salt until just blended. Do not over-mix. Add the apricots and raisins.

Place dough onto lightly floured surface and pat out to about one-inch high circle. Cut with floured round cutter, and place on parchment-lined cooking sheet.

Bake at 400°F for 8 to 10 minutes. Makes 15 scones.

Lemon and Poppy Seed Scone

2 cups all purpose flour
1/4 cup sugar
1/4 teaspoon salt
1 tsp baking powder
1/4 tsp baking soda
2 tablespoons poppy seeds
1 large egg
1/2 cup sour cream or plain yogurt
1 1/2 teaspoon lemon extract
1/2 cup butter, unsalted
1 to 2 tablespoons milk

Glaze:
1 cup powdered sugar
Lemon juice and a little lemon extract

Preheat oven to 400°F and line a cookie sheet with parchment paper. Mix together the flour, sugar, salt, baking powder, and baking soda. In a small bowl beat egg, then add the sour cream and lemon extract. Add the butter, cut into chunks, and use a pastry blender to have mixture resemble coarse breadcrumbs. Add the poppy seeds to the egg mixture, and then pour into the dry ingredients, and stir until soft dough forms.

Flour hands and surface, and turn dough out onto the floured surface. Knead about 5 or 6 times, and divide dough in half. Press dough into a circle about 3/4 or 1 inch thick. Cut each circle into 6 wedges and place on parchment paper.

Bake about 10 to 12 minutes until bottom of scone is lightly browned. Remove from cookie sheet to wire cooling rack. Makes 12 scones.

Glaze: mix powdered sugar, lemon extract, and lemon juice to make a thick glaze. Spread glaze onto cooled scone.

Everyone loves these scones and they are the perfect companions for the Ritz scones.

Mock clotted cream

2 cups whipping cream
3 tablespoons powdered sugar
3/4 cup sour cream

Put all ingredients into a chilled mixing bowl and beat with electric mixer until thick, and peaks form. Keep in refrigerator until ready to serve. This can be made a couple of hours before serving.

3rd Course ~ Sweets and Desserts

White Star Chocolate Raspberry Cakes

3/4 cup sugar
1/2 cup butter, softened
2 large eggs
1/4 cup evaporated milk
1 teaspoon vanilla extract
1 cup flour
1/4 teaspoon salt
1 cup fresh raspberries
1 12 oz package of chocolate chips
2 tablespoons powdered sugar
Preheat oven to 350° F.
Grease 10 muffin cups.

Beat sugar and butter in large mixing bowl until combined. Add eggs, evaporated milk, and vanilla extract; beat until blended. Stir in flour and salt. Gently fold in raspberries.

Spoon a heaping tablespoon of batter into prepared cups; place 1 tablespoon chocolate chips into each cup, pressing down slightly. Spoon another heaping tablespoon of batter over chocolate chips, covering completely.

Bake for 20 to 22 minutes or until cakes are golden brown around edges and top is set. Cool in pan on wire rack for 10 minutes. Run knife around edges to loosen; gently invert onto serving plate. Sprinkle with powdered sugar.

Victoria Sponge Cake

This cake is everyone's favorite. No leftovers when you serve this cake. Even the Queen can't resist.

Cake:

1 cup unsalted butter – room temperature
1 cup sugar
4 eggs, beaten
2 cups self-rising sifted flour

Filling:

1 cup of jams, preserves, or lemon curd.

Cream butter and sugar until light and fluffy, add eggs and mix well. Grease and line with parchment paper two 8-inch round cake tins. Divide batter between the pans and smooth the tops for evenness.

Bake 20 to 25 minutes at 375° F. Cool for 10 to 15 minutes in pans; then turn out onto wire racks to continue cooling.

Place a paper doily on footed cake plate. Sandwich bottoms of cake together with lemon curd, strawberry preserves, raspberry preserves, or apricot jam. Whipping cream can be used in place of the jams, or with the jams. Sprinkle top with powdered sugar and decorate cake plate with chemical-free flowers such as violets or nasturtiums. Wash the flowers well before use.

In a pinch, you can substitute a white cake mix!

Scottish Shortbread

Growing up, we never had tea without these wonderful cookies. My British friend Catherine gave me her recipe…one of the best!

2/3 cup unsalted butter, softened
1/4 cup powdered sugar
1 1/2 tablespoon sugar
Pinch of salt
1 1/2 cups all-purpose flour

Preheat the oven to 300°F. Lightly grease cookie sheet with butter.

With a fork, mix the sugars into the softened butter until thoroughly blended.

Gradually stir the flour and salt into the butter mixture, until thoroughly blended. If the dough is too dry, sprinkle a few drops of water over it, being careful not to over-moisten.

Roll out the mixture until it is about 1/4-inch thick. Cut with cookie cutters and gently place onto prepared sheet. Bake on the middle rack for about 45 minutes. Set your timer for 35 minutes. When lightly golden around edges, remove from oven and cool on pan for 5 minutes, then remove and place on wire cooling rack.

An Olympic Tea

The *Olympic* Specialty Restaurant on board the Celebrity Cruise Ship *Millenium* imparts a special romanticism that was part of the ceremony of being aboard the *Titanic.* The elegant and beautiful surroundings on such a luxurious vessel, complete with unsurpassed service from all the wait staff, affirmed one's status as a First-class passenger. The executive chef of the Celebrity Cruise Line recreated a menu for afternoon tea that might have had some of the very same items served on the *Titanic.* For variety, these recipes can be interchanged with the ones planned for the *Titanic Tea.*

1st Class Afternoon Olympic Tea

Sandwiches
Smoked Salmon and Chives
Roast Beef with Horseradish
Salami and Tapanade
Cucumber and Dill

Scones
Honey Raisin Scones
American Scones

Desserts
Olympic Cheesecake Tarts
Butterfly Cakes
Ginger Snap Stars

Teas

Jasmine

Earl Grey

Lapsang Souchoung

Recipes for an Olympic Tea

1st Course ~ Sandwiches

Smoked Salmon and Chives

8 oz cream cheese
2 tablespoons fresh chopped chives
1 lemon, zest and juice
Pinch of salt and pepper
36 slices smoked salmon
12 slices white bread

Spread softened cream cheese on one side of each bread slice. Mix chives with lemon, salt, and pepper. Place slices of salmon on half the bread slices; sprinkle chive mixture evenly over salmon, top with remaining slices. Trim crusts and cut into squares.

Cucumber and Dill

1/4 cup cream cheese
2 tablespoons plain yogurt
1/2 English cucumber (peeled and chopped)
1/4 cup mayonnaise
1 tablespoon lemon juice
2 tablespoon dill
Thin white bread

Blend yogurt, mayonnaise, lemon juice, dill and cucumbers. Spread softened cream cheese on bread slices. Spread cucumber mixture evenly over half of bread slices, then top with remaining slices. Trim crusts and cut into finger sandwiches.

Salami and Tapanade

1 clove garlic chopped
1 3/4 cup kalamata olives, chopped
2 oz can anchovies drained and chopped
2 tablespoon capers
1 teaspoon thyme chopped
1 teaspoon rosemary, chopped
3 teaspoon lemon juice
1/4 cup olive oil

Make a tapanade from all the above by mixing thoroughly.

Cut dark brown bread into rounds. Butter the bread to prevent bread from getting soggy. Place the tapanade on buttered bread and top with slice of salami. Serve open-face.

2nd Course ~ Scones

Honey Raisin Scones

2 oz golden raisins
8 oz all purpose flour
1 oz sugar
2 teaspoon baking powder
1 teaspoon sea salt
8 oz heavy cream
1 oz honey
Egg wash for top of scones before baking

Preheat oven to 425°F

Toss raisins with 2 oz flour, to prevent from sticking together. Place parchment paper onto cookie sheet.

Combine remaining flour with sugar, baking powder, and salt.

Add cream, honey and raisins.

Turn out onto floured surface and knead briefly and lightly.

Pat into a round one inch high, then cut into eight wedges. Place on parchment lined cookie sheet. Brush tops of scones with egg wash and sprinkle with scant amount of sugar.

Bake at 425°F for 12 minutes.

American Scones

2 eggs
1 1/2 cup milk
4 1/2 cup flour
3/4 cup sugar
3 tablespoons baking powder
3/4 teaspoon sea salt
1 1/4 cup butter, cubed

Combine 2 eggs, beaten with 1 1/2 cup whole milk. Combine flour, sugar, baking powder, and salt, then add butter and stir until blended and mixture resembles coarse breadcrumbs. Add egg mixture, stir until blended. When a soft dough has formed, turn out onto lightly floured surface and knead 4 to 5 times.

Cut with rounded floured cutters 1/2 inch thick. Place on lightly greased baking sheet, and bake at 400°F for 15 minutes.

Serve with clotted cream and jam.

3rd ~ Course Desserts

Berry-Cheesecake Tarts

Two frozen pie crusts

Filling:
8 oz cream cheese, softened
1/2 cup powdered sugar
1 tablespoon lemon juice
1/2 cup raspberry jelly
3 cups fresh raspberries or blackberries

Heat oven to 425°F. Cut each crust into five rounds with a four-inch cookie cutter. Fit each round over the back of muffin cup or inside tart pans; prick bottoms with a fork and bake at 425°F for seven to ten minutes, or until golden brown. Cool; remove from pans.

In small bowl, combine the cream cheese, powdered sugar, and lemon juice; beat until smooth and fluffy. Spoon 1 1/2 tablespoon cream cheese mixture into each tart shell. In medium pan over low heat, melt jelly. Remove from heat; stir in berries. Spoon over cream cheese filling. Refrigerate until serving time. Makes10 tarts.

Battenburg Cake

A surprise for everyone when you cut into this delightful and delicious treat. If cousin Rachel lived near me, I would have her bake this scrumptious checkerboard cake every week for Afternoon Tea. Rachel has a business making desserts (or Puds as they call them in England) called "Jolly Good Puds.com."

1 stick of unsalted butter
4 oz sugar
4 oz self-rising flour
1 teaspoon baking powder
2 eggs, beaten
Few drops of red food coloring
4 tablespoons seedless raspberry jam
4 tablespoons apricot jam

Almond Paste:
Few drops almond extract
4 oz extra fine sugar
4 oz icing sugar
4 oz ground almonds
2 egg yolks, plus a little egg white

Cover a piece of oblong cardboard to fit down the middle of an 8-inch square pan with foil. Grease the bottom and sides of the pan, including the cardboard divider with spray cooking oil.

Place the butter, sugar, flour, baking powder, and eggs in a bowl. Beat with an electric mixer until all the ingredients are blended, then beat for one more minute. Divide the cake mixture in half. To one half of the cake mixture, add red food coloring and mix until an even color is achieved. Spoon each mixture into half of the prepared cake pan and bake for 30 minutes or until firm.

Turn the cake out of the pan and cool on a wire rack.

Meanwhile, make almond paste by mixing dry ingredients together in a bowl; add egg yolks and almond extract, then add enough egg-white to make a stiff paste. Knead the mixture briefly until it comes together. Wrap the almond paste mixture in plastic wrap.

Cut each piece of cake in half (lengthways) to make 4 oblongs and trim any crusty edges off the cake pieces to even them up. Stack them together in a checkered pattern using the warmed raspberry jam to stick.

Roll out the almond paste on a large sheet of waxed paper, and sprinkled with sugar so it is long and wide enough to cover the four long sides of the cake (hold a piece of string around the cake to work out how long the paste needs to be) then brush the paste with warmed apricot jam.

Put the cake in the middle of the paste and press it around the cake so the join meets in the middle of one side (this is the bottom). Turn the cake the right way up and pinch along top two edges and lightly score diamonds to decorate. Cut a very thin slice off each end to neaten. Sprinkle with sugar.

Ginger Snap Stars

1/2 cup firmly packed brown sugar
1/4 cup butter
1 tablespoon cold water
1 cup plus 2 tablespoons all-purpose flour
2 tablespoons cornstarch
1/2 teaspoon cinnamon
1/8 teaspoon salt
1/4 cup sliced almonds

Beat sugar and butter with mixer until well blended. Add water and beat well. In another bowl, combine flour, cornstarch, cinnamon, and salt; add to butter mixture, beating until well blended. Gently press dough into a round disk, and wrap in plastic wrap and freeze for 30 minutes.

Preheat oven to 375°F

Remove plastic wrap from dough, and roll out to a thin 1/16 thickness on a floured surface. Cut with a 2-inch star-shaped cookie cutter. Place cookies on baking sheet; sprinkle with almonds.

Bake at 375°F for 8 minutes or until cookies are crisp and edges browned. Remove cookies from pan and cool on wire racks. Makes 4 dozen cookies.

"For tea, though ridiculed by those who are naturally coarse in their nervous sensibilities…will always be the favored beverage of the intellectual."
Thomas De Quincey

Chapter 8
Scones

Scones are traditional favorites served in the middle course of an Afternoon Tea and at a Cream Tea. Scones are normally served with strawberry or raspberry jam, and Devonshire cream. Homemade jams and jellies are even more special additions to the tea table.

Scones are best made the day of an event and eaten relatively soon after baking. Careful measuring, not too much kneading, keeping the dough on the moist side, and using a good quality soft-wheat flour, produces delectable scones. Pastry blenders to make preparation easier, are good investments.

Combining different teas with a variety of scones makes teatime more alluring. Strong teas are best paired with a more basic scone, as they offer less competition to the taste of the tea. Experiment, and most of all, enjoy!

Fruit Cream Scones

2 cups flour
1 tablespoon baking powder
1/2 teaspoon salt
1/4 cup sugar
1/2 cup chopped dried fruit (cranberries, mixed fruits, apricots)
1/4 cup raisins or sultanas

Stir above ingredients with a fork, and then add 1- 1/4-cup heavy cream.

Mix with fork, knead eight or nine times on lightly floured surface

Press out into a 10-inch circle.

Melt 3 tablespoons butter and add 1/4-cup sugar

Brush butter mixture over top of scones

Cut into wedges with floured knife and place on baking sheet, allowing an inch between the wedges.

Bake at 425°F for 15 minutes or until lightly browned. Cool and store in airtight container if not serving right away.

Blueberry Scones

2 cups flour
1/4 cup packed brown sugar
1 tablespoon baking powder
1/4 teaspoon salt
4 tablespoons cold butter, cut up
1-cup blueberries
2/3 cup heavy cream
1 large egg
1/2 tsp grated lemon peel

Preheat oven to 375°F

In large bowl, mix with fork: flour, sugar, baking powder, and salt. Cut butter into flour mixture with pastry blender until dry ingredients resemble coarse crumbs. Add blueberries, and toss lightly to mix ingredients.

In small bowl, mix with fork: cream, egg, and lemon peel, until blended. Slowly pour cream mixture into dry ingredients, and stir with spatula until a soft dough forms.

Lightly flour hands and knead dough in bowl until it comes together, only about 3 or 4 times; don't over-mix. Divide dough in half and on lightly floured surface, shape each half into a 6-inch round. With floured knife, cut each round into 6 wedges and transfer to an ungreased cooking sheet.

Bake for 22 to 25 minutes at 375° until golden brown. Serve warm with jam and clotted cream; or cool on rack. Makes 12 scones.

Sue's Scones

This recipe is from a dear friend and tea-sister from Zimbabwe. This is a good basic scone and can be eaten with any type of tea.

Preheat oven to 450°F.

Blend the following ingredients together with a pastry cutter to achieve the consistency of breadcrumbs:

2 cups self-rising flour
1/4 cup unsalted butter
2 tablespoons sugar

Mix in a separate bowl:

1 egg, beaten
1/3 cup buttermilk

Add egg mixture to dry ingredients and mix by cutting in with a knife, until ingredients come together. Knead a few times to form a dough. Handle dough as little as possible.

Place dough on lightly floured surface and pat out to about 3/4 inch thick. Brush with beaten egg. Bake at 450°F for 12 to 15 minutes.

Currant Scones

4 tablespoons unsalted butter
3 2/3 cups of flour
3 tablespoons sugar
1/4 teaspoon salt
2 teaspoons baking powder
1/3 cup currants
1 cup buttermilk
1 tablespoon vanilla extract

Preheat oven to 425°F

Sift flour and put into a large bowl. Add sugar, baking powder, and salt. Mix well with fork, then cut butter into the flour mixture with a pastry blender until it all resembles fine breadcrumbs. Add currants and a small amount of buttermilk to mixture, and stir a few times. Add vanilla and the rest of the buttermilk. Stir a few times with fork, then turn out onto a floured surface and knead 4 to 5 times. Pat out until dough is 1 1/2 to 2 inches thick.

Cut with a floured biscuit cutter and place on greased cookie sheet. Brush tops with an egg wash of 1 egg beaten with 1 tablespoon water. Bake 20 minutes until golden brown. Cool. Makes 8 to 10 scones.

Cherry Delight Scones

4 cups unsifted all-purpose flour
3 tablespoons sugar
4 teaspoons baking powder
1/2 teaspoon cream of tartar
1/2 teaspoon salt
3/4 cup butter
1 large egg
1 1/2 cups half and half
1/3 cup dried cherries

Heat oven to 425°F

Grease large baking sheet. In a large bowl, combine flour, 2 tablespoons sugar, baking powder, cream of tartar, and salt. With pastry blender, cut in butter until mixture resembles coarse crumbs. Separate egg, placing the egg white in a cup and the yolk into a small bowl. With fork, beat egg yolk, stir in half-and-half. Add yolk mixture to dry ingredients and mix lightly with a fork until mixture clings together and forms a soft dough.

Turn dough out onto lightly floured surface and knead gently 5 or 6 times. Gently knead in dried cherries. Divide dough into half, and roll out each half into 7-inch rounds, and cut each into 4 wedges. Place scones on cookie sheet, about 1-inch apart. Pierce tops with fork, then brush tops with egg white and sprinkle with remaining 1 tablespoon sugar. Bake for 15 to 18 minutes until golden brown. Makes 8 scones.

Rachel's Buttermilk Scones

My cousin Rachel lives in a lovely old stone cottage near Bath, England. She is one of the best cooks I know. You will love her scones.

2 1/4 cup self rising flour
1/3 cup sugar
1/2 cup butter, cold and cut into small pieces
6 oz buttermilk (or plain yogurt)

Put flour, sugar and butter into a large bowl and use a pastry blender until it resembles fine breadcrumbs. Make a well and add the buttermilk into the center of the well. Mix lightly with a fork until a soft dough is formed. Don't mix too much or the dough gets tough. Turn out onto a lightly floured surface and knead very briefly and lightly.

Roll or press dough out to approximately 1-inch thick and cut into 2-inch rounds with a floured cutter, dipping the cutter in flour after each cut. Try not to twist the cutter, or the scones will be lopsided. Gather trimmings and repeat until all dough used.

Transfer to lightly greased baking sheet, spaced a little apart. Brush with milk or beaten egg and bake at 375°F for 15 minutes, just until lightly brown.

Strawberry and Pepper Scones

I never would have guessed how tasty these scones could be. Try them...they take a little longer, but worth it!

Heat oven to 250°F

Wash, hull and chop 1 cup of strawberries into small pieces.

Place them on parchment-lined cookie sheet, and sprinkle them with 2 teaspoons sugar. Roll strawberries to make sure they are covered evenly. Bake for 30 minutes, remove from oven and sprinkle with 1 -1/2 tsp black pepper. Let cool.

2 cups flour
1/4 cup sugar
2 teaspoons baking powder
1/2 teaspoon baking soda
1/2 teaspoon salt
1/4 cup butter
2/3 cup sour cream
1 large egg

Mix flour, sugar, powder, soda, and salt together, add butter and blend with a pastry cutter until the mixture resembles fine bread-crumbs. Add strawberries and mix into dry mixture. Add sour cream and egg, and blend until mixed. Turn out onto lightly floured surface and knead lightly, 5 or 6 times. Roll or pat out to about 3/4 inch thick and cut with a floured cookie cutter into rounds or hearts.

Place onto parchment-lined cookie sheets and brush their tops with milk. Bake for about 15 minutes. Serve warm with clotted cream.

Orange Currant Scones

3-1/2 cups flour
3/4 cup sugar
2-1/2 teaspoons baking powder
1/2 teaspoon baking soda
3/4 cup butter
3/4 cups currants soaked in orange liqueur or orange juice
1 cup buttermilk

Preheat oven to 425°F

In a large bowl, combine flour, sugar, powder, soda, and salt until thoroughly blended. I use a whisk for this.

With a pastry cutter, cut in butter into flour mixture until it resembles coarse breadcrumbs. Drain the currants and add them to the flour mixture. Add buttermilk and stir with a fork until a dough is formed. Flour hands and gather dough together and gently knead with your hands. Turn out onto a floured surface and gently knead, adding more flour if needed.

Roll or pat into a circle about 1/2-inch thick. Using a floured cookie cutter, cut into shapes. Bake on lightly greased baking sheet. Brush tops of scones with cream and sprinkle with sugar. Bake 20 to 30 minutes until tops are lightly browned. Serve warm. Makes 30 scones.

Microwave Lemon Curd

4 ounces lemon juice
4 eggs, beaten
1 stick (4 ounces) butter
2 1/4 cups sugar

Mix the lemon juice and sugar in a glass mixing bowl and stir well, then add the butter to the mixture. Place the bowl into the microwave oven and cook on high for two minutes. Stir well. Repeat cooking on high until butter is melted, check often so as not to burn the mixture.

Take the bowl out of the microwave and slowly add in the beaten eggs, using a wire whisk. Place the mixture back into the microwave and continue cooking on medium at one-minute intervals. Beat with whisk after each minute, then continue to cook and stir until the mixture is at the consistency of thickened pudding. The lemon curd will continue to thicken as it cools. Place into clean jar and refrigerate.

I love lemon curd on English muffins, but it is equally as good on scones, used in place of jam. Blending cooled lemon curd with equal parts of whipping cream, is another use for lemon curd, by adding the mixture to cooled tart shells.

Lemon curd will last about a week in your refrigerator.

Mock Clotted Cream #1

1/2 cup sour cream
2 cups heavy whipping cream

Add one drop of yellow food coloring to whipping cream. Beat cream until very stiff. Gradually blend in sour cream. Store and serve in glass containers. Serve with warm scones.

Mock Clotted Cream #2

2 cups heavy whipping cream with one to two drops of yellow food coloring
2 tablespoons sugar added just when the cream begins to thicken.

Beat until stiff peaks form when beaters are lifted.

Tips for whipping cream: Use heavy whipping cream, which has sufficient fat to thicken properly. Thoroughly chill the bowl and the beaters beforehand. Use an electric mixer, and increase the speed as the cream begins to thicken. Do not over-whip, or the cream will separate into butter and whey. Store in glass containers for best results. Whipped cream can be made several hours before serving, best kept refrigerated.

"Real" Devonshire or Cornish clotted cream is made from unpasturized milk from cows in the southern coastal area of England. The cream has a yellowish hue, and is very thick and rich. Milk is heated until a thick layer of cream is formed on the surface, and then cooled. This process takes about 24 hours. The finished product is so thick that is doesn't need whipping. Devonshire cream is imported and can be bought in specialty markets, such as Fresh Market, Whole Foods, Trader Joe's, and in some tearooms. There is nothing quite like big dollops of clotted cream on warm-from-the-oven scones!

Every year I lead a "Taste of Britain Tea Tour," that includes stops at wonderful places for Afternoon Tea. A Georgian farmhouse, owned by Prince Charles, is reminiscent of something in a Jane Austen novel. It is one of the favorite places to have tea. Large bowls of real clotted cream adorn the tables...and wreck havoc with our waistbands!

Baking Tips

- Use unsalted butter for baking, so to not lose control of the amount of salt in a recipe.
- Don't substitute margarine for butter. Margarine contains more water than oil, and might yield undesirable results. To soften butter quickly, slice into small pieces and heat in a microwave a few seconds.
- To accurately measure dry ingredients, scoop and level. Dip measuring spoon into sugar, baking powder, baking powder, etc., scoop up the ingredient, then level off the top with the flat edge of a knife. When measuring flour, avoid scooping, but, instead, use a spoon to place the flour into the measuring cup to keep measurement accurate, then level with the flat edge of a knife.
- Be sure your baking powder and baking soda are fresh and active so they can leaven the dough. Most containers are marked with a "use by" date. Test the baking powder to see if it fizzes when you drop half a teaspoon into a cup of warm water. For baking soda, be sure it bubbles and fizzes when a few drops of lemon juice or vinegar are added to a small amount of the soda.
- Baking soda starts acting as soon as it is combined with a liquid. If it is the leavening agent in the recipe, get the item into the oven as fast as possible. Baking powder, on the other hand, must be heated first.

- For best flavor and aroma, use pure vanilla extract, not imitation.
- Use the right size egg in a recipe. The wrong size can make dough too wet or dry and affect the texture of the finished product.
- Cool your baking sheets thoroughly prior to adding more dough or you otherwise risk affecting the texture of the scone or cookie.
- An easy way to grease a baking sheet is to use the butter wrapper and wipe the leftover butter across the baking sheet, or run the stick of butter across the sheet.
- Cookie sheets: Buy the right one – shiny, heavy-gauge sheets with low or no sides, are best. Avoid black or dark cookie sheets as they cause items to bake faster and brown too much. Insulated sheets yield pale cookies with soft centers; if you bake until the cookies or scones are brown, they will probably be too dry. Cheap pans do not conduct heat well and warp when subjected to high heat.
- Metal pans brown more evenly than do glass.
- Baking on parchment paper makes removal of cookies, and clean-up easier.
- Always preheat the oven.
- Always use a timer.

The secret of really good scones is to work the dough quickly and lightly, kneading very little, then eat the baked scones with clotted cream and jam as soon as possible! Someone has to do it!

"Taste and see that the Lord is good."
Psalm 34:8

Chapter 9

Tea Sandwiches "101"

Tips for Easy Sandwich Making

- Use thin or sandwich bread – a mix of wheat and white. Pullman loaves ordered from a bakery, work well. Try making your own bread and add food coloring with the liquid before the mixing. This is unique for bridal and baby showers.
- One normal loaf of bread will make about 40 small tea sandwiches.
- Make each kind of sandwich the same shape. Such as: egg salad -- square; chicken -- triangle; cucumber –- fingers.
- Freeze the loaf of bread before making the sandwiches.
- Seal bread's surfaces with either butter or cream cheese to prevent the sandwiches from becoming soggy.
- Apply moderate amount of filling for sandwich, not too thick.
- Trim crusts after making sandwiches. Use an electric knife.
- After making sandwiches, cover with a damp paper towel or lettuce leaves, then place in sealed containers in the refrigerator. Keep a damp paper towel over the sandwiches when placed on serving dishes until ready to eat. Sandwiches without crusts dry out quickly.

Recipes

Deviled Ham

1 small can deviled ham
1/4 cup finely chopped green onion
1 tablespoon Dijon mustard

Combine all ingredients and spread on buttered slices of wheat bread.

Trim crusts and cut into desired shapes.

Curried Chicken

2 cups of cooked and chopped chicken breasts (or 1 large can of canned chicken, drained)
1/4 cup mayonnaise
2 green onions, finely chopped
1/2 teaspoon or more of curry powder
1/4 cup chopped cashews

Mix all of the above and spread on buttered bread of your choice. Trim the crusts and cut into desired shapes.

Cucumber

Wash and slice one English hothouse cucumber as thin as possible. Place in colander and sprinkle with a little rice vinegar and salt. Place a plate on top of cucumbers to weigh it down. Let drain and press out remaining liquid on paper towels. Spread white bread with 8 oz of softened cream cheese that has been mixed with 1 teaspoon of horseradish. Place cucumber slices on one slice of bread, then top with second slice of bread. Trim crusts and cut into finger-shaped sandwiches.

Cotswold Cheddar

1 cup sharp cheddar cheese, shredded
1/2 cup mayonnaise
1/3 cup finely chopped pecans
1 tablespoon finely chopped onion
3 strips well-cooked bacon, drained and crumbled

Combine all ingredients and refrigerate one hour.

Spread butter onto wheat bread, place cheese spread onto bread, and then top with other slice of bread. Cut into desired shapes.

Village Cheese and Pickle

1 cup finely shredded extra sharp cheddar cheese
1/4 cup mayonnaise
1/3 cup chopped Branston Pickle (available in international sections of grocery stores)

Branston Pickle is a combination of diced vegetables in a spicy sauce. It is one of Britain's popular delicacies and is perfect for a menu item that needs a little spice!

Combine all ingredients and refrigerate for one hour before making into sandwiches. Butter bread of your choice, spread with the cheese filling, and cut into desired shapes after trimming crusts.

Curry Cheese Sandwiches

Curry powder 1/4 to 1/2 teaspoon
4 oz cream cheese
2 tablespoons orange marmalade
Garnish: coconut, chopped peanuts, and chopped green onion.

Mix curry with cream cheese and marmalade. Top with coconut, chopped peanuts and green onion. Great on pumpernickel or other brown bread. Cut into squares or triangles. Serve as open-face sandwiches.

Egg Salad Sandwiches

6 hard boiled eggs, finely chopped
1/4 cup fine chopped green onion
1/4 cup sweet pickle relish
1/3 cup mayonnaise
1/2 teaspoon salt
1/4 teaspoon pepper

Combine all ingredients well. Chill, then spread thinly on buttered slices of bread. Trim crusts and cut into desired shapes.

Ginger and Carrot Sandwiches

4 grated carrots
4 tablespoons cream cheese
4 tablespoons mayonnaise
2 teaspoons grated stem ginger (available in jars)
Salt and pepper to taste
Several small leaves of Rocket (arugula lettuce)
8 slices Rye bread

Mix the carrots, cheese, mayonnaise, and ginger until well blended. Add the salt, pepper, and rocket salad leaves.

Butter each piece of bread with softened butter. Spread the carrot mixture evenly over half the bread slices, then top with remaining slices. Remove the crusts and cut into desired shapes.

Ham and Cheese

8 oz cream cheese
1 cup sour cream
1 1/2 cups grated cheddar cheese
3 chopped green onions, chopped
3 teaspoons Worcestershire sauce
4 oz chopped ham

Mix cream cheese and sour cream.

Add additional ingredients and mix until well blended.

Spread on buttered wheat sandwich bread, trim crusts and cut into desired shape.

Horseradish and Roast Beef

2 tablespoons mayonnaise
1 teaspoon prepared horseradish
8 thin slices Pepperidge Farm white sandwich bread
1/4 lb. roast beef, sliced paper-thin
Thin sliced provolone cheese
Salt and freshly ground pepper, to taste

Stir together the mayonnaise and horseradish, and spread on one side of each bread slice. Layer the roast beef and cheese on the bread slices, and season with salt and pepper. Top with the remaining bread slices.

Trim the crusts and cut the sandwiches into quarters. Makes 16 tea sandwiches.

Sometimes it is nice to have a little surprise added to the sandwich course in the form of a vegetable "cup." They are bite-size and an added dimension to your tea menu.

Cucumber Cups

2 English cucumbers (seeded)
1 8-oz. package cream cheese, softened
1/3 cup finely chopped onion
1 tablespoon snipped fresh dill
1 tablespoon milk
1/8 teaspoon salt
1/8 teaspoon pepper
Toppings:
Chopped nuts
Finely chopped chives
Lemon zest

Peel cucumbers; cut each crosswise into 2-inch thick chunks. Using a spoon or melon baller, hollow one end of each chunk; set aside.

In a small bowl, combine the cream cheese, onion, dill, salt, and pepper; spoon this mixture into the hollowed cucumbers, mounding just slightly. Sprinkle on the toppings.

Refrigerate until serving. Makes 16.

Cherry Tomato Cups

24 cherry tomatoes
6 – oz herbed goat cheese
2 tablespoons fresh-snipped chives

Allow goat cheese to stand at room temperature for 30 minutes to soften. Slice off the bottoms of the tomatoes so they are flat. Cut a large slice from the stem end, then hollow out the tomato with a spoon or melon baler. Place the tomatoes upside down on paper towel to drain for several minutes.

Spoon cheese into the tomatoes, mounding slightly. Sprinkle the tops with the chives.

Cover and chill for up to 24 hours. Serves 12

"I believe it is customary in good society to take some slight refreshment at five o'clock."
Oscar Wilde

Chapter 10
Tea Time Desserts

Sweet Success

There is a saying...life is uncertain - eat dessert first,
but at an Afternoon Tea, we say...tea is never complete,
without the sweets!
Bon Appetit

Earl Grey Tea Cake

8 oz dried fruit
8 oz of strong Earl Grey tea
2 tablespoons melted butter
2 cups bran cereal
1/3-cup sugar
2 large eggs, slightly beaten
1 cup of self-rising flour, sifted

Preheat oven to 350°F.

Grease a loaf pan

Mix bran and fruit in a large bowl. Pour the tea over the fruit and bran, and let sit for ten minutes. Stir in the other ingredients and mix well. Pour the batter into a well-greased loaf pan, and bake for 35 to 40 minutes

Allow the cake to cool in the pan, then when cool, take the cake out of the pan and finish cooling on a wire rack. Slice the cake and serve with a generous spread of cream cheese or butter.

This cake keeps well in an airtight container.

Angela's Tea Cake

Cousin Angela always has this cake in her cake-tin. She has been my sidekick on many of the "Taste of Britain Tea Tours," and graciously provided Sunday lunch in her lovely, Somerset home near Bath, England.

2 cups butter, softened
1-1/2 cups sugar
2 cups flour
4 eggs
1 lb of chopped dried fruit (currants, raisins, sultanas, cherries, etc.)
1 to 2 teaspoons of cinnamon
1/2 to 1 teaspoon cloves
1/2 to 1 cup chopped nuts (if desired)

Preheat oven to 350°F

Cream the butter and sugar together until smooth. Add the eggs, one at a time just prior to adding the last egg, stir in 1/4 cup flour, then continue to add the rest of the flour and spices after adding the last egg. Stir in the fruit (and nuts) and mix with a spoon until well blended.

Pour cake batter into a parchment-lined spring-release pan.

Bake at 350°F for 2 hours. Cool on rack thoroughly, then remove from pan.

Store in an airtight container.

This cake is rich and moist and goes extremely well with a nice cup of Darjeeling or Earl Grey Tea.

Honey Lace Delights

These delicate lacy cookies are easy and so delicious, but you have to work quickly. Have ready two cookie sheets lined with parchment paper before beginning.

2 tablespoons unsalted butter
2 tablespoons brown sugar
1-1/2 tablespoons honey
2 tablespoons flour
Pinch of salt

Preheat oven to 375°F

Line two large cookie sheets with parchment paper, then set aside.

In a small pan, melt the butter, sugar, and honey until the butter is melted. Remove the pan from the heat and whisk in the flour and the salt. Continue whisking until the batter is smooth.

Here is the "work quickly part!" Drop 1/2-teaspoon of batter onto the prepared cookie sheets, three to four inches apart. Bake the cookies until they spread out and turn a golden brown, about 5 to 6 minutes. Watch carefully, as they can burn easily.

Transfer the cookies to a wire cooling rack and let them cool completely. These cookies are delicate, so handle gently with your fingers as you place them on serving dishes. Because they are so fragile, place them in a safe place away from little hands!

Chocolate-Dipped Lemon Cookies

Every tea party needs a little chocolate. These cookies are wonderful and a good choice if you don't want a lot of chocolate, just a taste!

10 tablespoons chilled unsalted butter (1 stick plus 2 tablespoons) cut into 8 to 10 pieces.

1-1/2 cups of cake flour

1 cup powdered sugar

1 teaspoon lemon juice

1 medium lemon zest (only the yellow part; the white is bitter)

4 oz dark chocolate (dipping or coating chocolate, melted per package directions, can be bought in craft stores or in grocery stores often near the strawberries)

Using a food processor with the metal blade, blend butter, flour, and sugar until it reaches a consistency of coarse breadcrumbs. Add lemon juice and the lemon zest and continue mixing until it becomes a ball.

Remove the dough from the food processor and flatten into a round shape. Cut the dough into fourths and roll each piece into a log, about 4 to 5 inches long. Wrap each log in plastic wrap and place into freezer.

When ready to bake, preheat oven to 325°F and cut the logs into 1/2 inch slices and place on ungreased cookie sheet. Bake for about 15 minutes or until the cookie is slightly puffed and bottoms are a light brown. Remove from oven and place cookie sheet on a wire cooling rack.

Line a cookie sheet with waxed paper. When the cookies are cool, dip each cookie halfway into the melted chocolate and place on the waxed paper so the chocolate can harden. Makes 36 cookies.

Macaroon Tarts

My husband loves coconut. This is one of his favorites!

1 1/2 cups unsweetened coconut
2 large egg whites
1/4 cup sugar
1/2 cup heavy cream
1/2 cup lemon curd

Heat oven to 350°F
Spray mini-muffin tins with cooking spray.

In a large bowl, combine the coconut, egg whites, and sugar. Mix until the mixture holds together when you squeeze it with your hands. Take enough of the mixture to form a ball about the size of a walnut. Place inside the muffin tins and use your thumb to made a hollow area in the center and make a little crust on the top.

Bake the crusts until they are golden brown, about 10 to 12 minutes. Watch carefully, because coconut burns easily. Remove from oven and let the crusts cool slightly. Turn the crust onto a wire rack and continue cooling.

Whip the cream until stiff. Gently fold in the lemon curd and fill each crust with the whipped cream mixture. Garnish with lemon zest. Keep chilled until ready to serve.

Makes 8 to 10.

Butterfly Cakes

Children love these little cakes, and they also love to help make them!

1 Lemon or Butter-cream cake mix
4 eggs
1- 4 oz vanilla or lemon instant pudding mix
3/4 - cup water
1/3 - cup water

Filling
1/2-pound softened butter
1 pound powdered sugar
A few drops of lemon extract
Beat butter, sugar, and the lemon extract until creamy.

Preheat oven to 350°F

Spray cupcake pans (24 normal or 80 mini cupcakes) with baking spray.

Beat the eggs until mixed well, then add the cake mix and pudding mix; and beat on medium speed for about 5 minutes. Fill cupcake pans 2/3 full and bake normal-sized as directed on cake mix box; mini-cupcakes for 10 to 15 minutes.

Cool and remove from pans. Cut off the top of the cupcakes and scoop out a little bit of the cake to leave a small hollow. Cut the top into two parts. Place the filling into the hollow, and place the "wings" cut side down to resemble butterfly wings. Sprinkle with powdered sugar.

Pavlova with Strawberries and Cream

Several ladies from the "Taste of Britain" tea tours requested that this recipe be part of the dessert section, as they loved it so much.

3 large egg whites
1/4 teaspoon cream of tartar
1/4 teaspoon salt
1 teaspoon vanilla extract
1/2 cup sugar

Preheat oven to 275°F
Line cookie sheet with parchment paper.
Draw eight 3-inch circles on the parchment paper.

In a large bowl, beat the egg whites with mixer at high speed, gradually add in cream of tartar and salt until egg whites begin to mound. Continue beating at high speed and add vanilla and sugar, sprinkling in one tablespoon of sugar at a time, making sure the sugar is completely dissolved after each addition. Egg whites should stand in stiff and glossy peaks when the beaters are lifted.

Spoon meringue mixture inside the circles on the parchment paper. With a spoon, shape and spread meringue into a "nest" with the sides about 1-1/2 inch high.

Bake meringue shells about 1 hour and fifteen minutes. Turn off the oven and allow the meringue to remain in the oven for one hour to dry out. Transfer the meringue shells to a wire rack and cool completely.

The meringue can be made a day ahead and stored in an airtight container. Do not fill until ready to serve.

Filling:
1 pint heavy whipping cream, whipped until stiff peaks form
Fresh strawberries washed and hulled.

Just before serving, place the meringues on a large serving plate and fill with whipped cream. Top with strawberries or other fresh fruit.

Earlier in the book I mentioned that I like to cook more than I like to bake. Our local bakery is a wonderful source for the items that I may not have time to bake, or to add a special dessert that will wow guests. Each Afternoon Tea can have 2 or 3 desserts or sometimes, depending on who my guests are, I may only serve 1 or 2. I know the *Titanic* Teas were abundant with sweet offerings, so you can be extravagant in this part of the tea service.

"Gracious words are like a honeycomb, sweetness to the soul and health to the body."
Proverbs 16:24

Chapter 11

High Tea

High Tea…the words suggest an elegant and grand affair. However, the "high" in this tea is a simple dinner, or supper, at a high table, not a coffee table or a low table in the living room. Not "high" toned, but very basic.

Third-class passengers on the *Titanic* were served their "tea" or evening meal in the dining rooms on Deck F. The *Titanic* provided two dining rooms in steerage, with a joint capacity of 473 passengers per seating. As there were more than 700 third-class passengers on this maiden voyage, two seatings were necessary. The *Titanic* was the first ocean liner ever to offer steerage passengers full dining privileges. Previously, and on competing ship lines, third-class passengers were required to bring their own food or eating utensils. This new policy of the White Star Lines was intended to increase their third-class bookings.

These dining rooms were pleasantly decorated with simple, white furniture. Long rows of banquet-style tables for 16 to 20 persons were covered with linen tablecloths. The passengers were served on the special White Star china with the ship's logo, a red flag, in the center of the dishes. The passengers were provided with hot evening meals, a pleasant ending to the day. And of course, it would have included a pot of tea to complement the meal.

High tea can be a delightful new custom for you to try. Your friends will be pleasantly surprised by the variety of menu offerings provided. Think of this as an informal dinner party, with both men and women enjoying the casual style of dining.

I love to give High Teas, all times of the year, as it is a quick and simple meal that can be prepared with a minimum of advance planning. The meal can include several or more of the menu items, followed by a dessert. The hot tea choices are wide-open, and can include decaffeinated teas if your guests prefer no caffeine. The time for a High Tea is usually after 5:00 p.m. and can be a prelude to an evening of games, or attending a movie or play.

Table settings should include a tablecloth or placemats and linen napkins, plus your nice teacups or tea-mugs. High Tea is not necessarily a step-down dining option, just a more relaxed and casual affair.

Several years ago I wanted to host an Afternoon Tea for a bridal shower. However, the guests could not come in the afternoon, so a High Tea was planned for the evening. I had reservations about not having a "proper Afternoon Tea," as one of the guests was married to a social diplomat. They traveled extensively in Great Britain and I wanted everything to be perfect. I needlessly worried, as the tea was a wonderful alternative.

Savory Course

Choose one or two of the following savory recipes for the first-course. A fresh-fruit salad is a nice addition to these dishes.

Scotch Eggs

A real savory dish. Once you have tried them at your High Tea, it will be a favorite. The combination of sausage and eggs in a new presentation is always fun to try. My mother made this recipe by frying the eggs and sausage. This one, by baking, is much quicker… and eliminates many calories!

1-pound pork sausage
1 tablespoon fresh chopped chives or green onion.
Salt and pepper to taste
12 small hard boiled eggs, peeled
Flour for coating
2 eggs, beaten
1 1/2 cups breadcrumbs

Mix sausage, chives, salt, and pepper.

Divide into 12 portions. On a floured surface, flatten sausage mixture into a round circle. Dust eggs with flour. Place beaten eggs into a small bowl and the breadcrumbs into another bowl. Place each egg on a circle of sausage, mold the sausage around the egg, sealing seams well with water. Roll each sausage-covered egg in beaten egg, then into the breadcrumbs. Place onto a cookie sheet.

Bake the eggs in the oven at 400°F for 30 minutes or until sausage is well done. Drain onto the paper towel. To prevent the eggs from rolling on the baking sheet, place a toothpick through the bottom of the eggs at an angle.

Toad In the Hole

Don't let this old English name discourage you from trying this tasty and easy dish. My mother made this often for our tea when we were growing up.

1-1/2 pounds link sausage (try low-fat)
2 eggs
1 cup flour
1/2 teaspoon salt
1/4 teaspoon pepper
2 cups milk

Brown the sausages and place them in an oblong 11 x 7 greased baking dish. Place the sausage links evenly apart in the pan, so the batter can go between the sausages. Mix the eggs, flour, salt, pepper, and milk, mix well with a rotary beater or whisk, and pour over the sausage. As it bakes, the "heads" of some of the sausage will poke up thru the batter. Bake for 30 minutes, cut into 6 or 8 pieces and serve.

Cottage Pie

Here is a recipe that is so simple and good. My friend Margaret gave me this timesaving recipe. It is very similar to Shepherd's Pie.

1 lb lean ground beef
1 medium onion, chopped
6 medium to large carrots, peeled and chopped
1/2 teaspoon Marmite or Vegemite (this is optional, but can be found in specialty stores)
1/3 cup tomato paste
1 vegetable or beef bouillon cube, dissolved in 1/4 cup boiling water
4 oz chopped tomatoes (can use canned)
Salt and pepper to taste
4 cups mashed potatoes (previously cooked and warmed)

In a frying pan, brown onions until soft, not browned. Add ground beef and brown with the onions until beef turns brown. Add carrots, Marmite, tomato paste, bouillon, tomatoes, salt, and pepper. Simmer for 1/2 hour, then place into a greased casserole dish.

Mash the potatoes with a little milk to make them soft. Place the mashed potatoes on top of the beef mixture and bake at 300°F for 15 minutes. Sprinkle some grated Parmesan cheese on top and broil until light brown.

Scones

Irish Potato Scones

Instead of serving the scones with Devonshire cream and jam, use butter and jam.

2 cups flour
1 teaspoon cream of tartar
1 teaspoon baking soda
1/2 teaspoon salt
2 teaspoons sugar
1/2 cup butter, softened
1/4 cup cold mashed potatoes (made without butter or milk)
3/4 cup milk or buttermilk
Cream for topping

Sift the dry ingredients into a large bowl, then cut in the butter and potatoes with a pastry blender. Stir in the flour; then add the milk and mix gently. If dough is too sticky, add more flour.

Place dough onto lightly floured surface and pat to 3/4 inch thick. Cut with a cookie cutter into desired shapes; dip the cutter into flour after each use. Brush tops lightly with cream. Bake on ungreased cookie sheet for 12 to 15 minutes at 400°F.

Cheese Scones

Scones that aren't so sweet go best with High Tea.

With this easy recipe, you'll have hot, delicious scones ready in minutes.

2 cups Original Bisquick® brand mix
1/3 cup sharp cheddar cheese, shredded
3 tablespoons sugar
1/3 cup whipping (heavy) cream
1 egg
2 tablespoons milk
2 tablespoons sugar

Heat oven to 425°F. Grease a cookie sheet.

Mix Bisquick, cheese, sugar, whipping cream, and egg until soft dough forms. Turn dough onto lightly floured surface. Roll the dough into the flour to coat. Shape the dough into a ball and knead gently 8 to 10 times.

Flour hands and pat dough into an 8-inch circle on cookie sheet. Brush dough with milk; sprinkle with 2 tablespoons sugar. Cut into 8 wedges, but do not separate.

Bake at 425°F about 12 minutes or until golden brown; carefully separate wedges. Serve warm.

Barmbrack Style Earl Grey Tea Loaf

I like this bread, because its texture and inclusion of chopped dried fruit makes it reminiscent of Barmbrack, an Irish bread that's often an accompaniment for High Tea. The addition of Earl Grey Tea gives it a nice pleasant taste.

8 ounces of chopped dried fruit
2 cups of bran cereal
1 cup of strong Earl Grey tea
1/2 cup sugar
2 tablespoons melted butter
2 large eggs, lightly beaten
1 cup of self-rising flour, sifted

Preheat oven to 350°F. Grease a loaf pan.

Mix together the dried fruit and bran cereal. Pour the tea into the fruit mixture; let stand for 10 minutes. Stir in the other ingredients until well blended. Pour into a well-greased loaf pan and bake for 35 to 40 minutes.

Allow the bread to cool before turning out of pan. Serve sliced with butter or cream cheese. 8 servings

Desserts

A High Tea can also include some assorted cheeses, crackers, and sliced fruit, served in place of dessert. The cheese, crackers, and fruit could also be served with the savory course.

English Trifle

When I was a child, we begged mother to make this trifle. It is not the traditional trifle that you might have made before, but it is the perfect ending to a High Tea.

1 large package Jell-O, any flavor -made as directed on package – do not set.
1 large package vanilla pudding or Birds English Custard -made as directed on package.
1 angel food cake or sponge cake
1 large can fruit cocktail, drained
2 cups whipping cream, whipped
Maraschino cherries for garnish

Cut cake into 1-inch squares and place them in the bottom of a trifle bowl. Pour liquid Jell-O over the cake pieces, followed by the fruit cocktail, and blend very gently. Refrigerate until the Jell-O is set. Spread cooled custard or pudding over Jell-O combination, and top with the whipped cream. Decorate with the cherries.

Lemon Coconut Poppy Seed Cake

Our friend John won't come to tea unless I bake this cake!

1 package lemon cake mix
1 small package instant lemon pudding mix (not sugar free)
1 cup sour cream
1/2 cup oil
4 eggs
1/2 cup water
1 teaspoon coconut extract (add to water)
1/3 cup poppy seeds

Preheat oven to 350° F

Grease a bundt pan thoroughly with baking cooking spray

Mix cake mix, pudding mix, sour cream, oil, eggs, water and coconut extract in large mixing bowl, then beat on medium speed for 2 minutes. Fold in poppy seeds, and pour into prepared bundt pan.

Bake at 350° F for 50 to 60 minutes.

Cool in pan for 15 minutes, then place cake upside down on cake plate.

Dust with powdered sugar slice and serve when cool. Add some fresh raspberries for an added treat.

Oatmeal Jam Slices

These are a quick and delicious treat.

Preheat oven to 375°F
Grease an 11 by 7-inch pan

1-1/2 cups flour
1 teaspoon baking powder
1/4 teaspoon salt
1-1/2 cups rolled oats
1 cup brown sugar
3/4 cup butter
3/4 cup fruit preserves (apricot, cherry, plum, peach, etc.)

Place flour, baking powder, salt, oats, and brown sugar into a food processor with the metal blade and give it a few pulses. The oatmeal should be medium fine, but not ground.

Add the butter and pulse until the mixture looks like course breadcrumbs.

Pat 2/3 of the crumb mixture into the greased 11 by 7- inch pan. Spread the fruit preserves evenly on top of the flour mixture, then top with the remaining crumbs and pat down a little - don't flatten -just pat so it isn't loose.

Bake at 375°F for 35 minutes. Cool completely on wire rack, then cut into 24 slices.

Sticky Toffee Pudding

Another favorite!

1/3 cup butter
3/4 cup sugar
2 eggs, beaten
1 cup self-rising flour
6 oz chopped and sugared rolled dates, pitted
1/4 cup chopped pecans
1 teaspoon vanilla
2 teaspoons made strong coffee
1 teaspoon baking soda

Sauce:
1 stick butter
6 tablespoons heavy cream
1 cup packed brown sugar

First make the sauce:

Place all sauce ingredients into a saucepan and heat very gently, stirring frequently, until the sugar has melted and all the crystals are dissolved. Pour about half the sauce into a well-buttered 11 by 7-inch pan to cover the bottom of the pan.

Next, make the pudding:

Place the chopped dates into a bowl and pour 6 oz of boiling water over the dates. Add the vanilla, coffee, the soda, and set aside.

In a large bowl, cream the butter and sugar with an electric mixer until pale and fluffy. Gradually add the eggs, beating well after each egg. Carefully fold in the sifted flour, using a large spoon, and then fold in the date mixture, including the liquid and the nuts. The mixture will look very runny at this stage. Pour the mixture into the pan over the sauce. Bake in a preheated 350°F oven about 45 minutes or until firm to touch. A toothpick should come out clean.

Cool for 5 minutes and then heat up the remaining toffee sauce. Run a knife around the edges and pour the remaining warm sauce over the pudding. Enjoy!

"She found a cloth and laid the tea, setting out cakes and biscuits, sugar bowl and silver milk jug. Even for kitchen tea, it appeared, her standards were meticulous."
Rosamunde Pilcher *"The Day of the Storm"*

Nearer, my God, to Thee

The last words heard from the *Titanic* as the band played. This was reported by Mrs. W. J. Douton, a survivor whose husband drowned.

Nearer, My God, to Thee
Sarah Flower Adams
19th Century Hymn

Nearer, My God, to Thee,
Nearer to Thee!
E'en though it be a cross
That raiseth me;
Still all my song shall be
Nearer, my God to Thee,
Nearer to Thee!

Though like the wandered,
The sun gone down,
Darkness be over me,
My rest a stone;
Yet in my dreams I'd be
Nearer, my God, to Thee,
Nearer to Thee!

There let the way appear
Steps unto heaven;
All that thou sendest me
In mercy given;
Angels to beckon me,
Nearer, my God, to Thee,
Nearer to Thee!

Then with my waking thoughts,
Bright with thy praise,
Out of my stony griefs
Bethel I'll raise;
So by my woes to be
Nearer, my God, to Thee,
Nearer to Thee!

Or if on joyful wing
Cleaving the sky,
Sun, moon and stars forgot,
Upward I fly;
Still all my song shall be
Nearer, my God, to Thee,
Nearer to Thee.

CPSIA information can be obtained at www.ICGtesting.com
Printed in the USA
BVOW030639170513

320954BV00004B/8/P

9 781432 791995